# Essentials of

# PSYCHOLOGICAL ASSESSMENT
## Series

**Everything you need to know to administer, interpret, and score the major psychological tests... the quick-reference guides written by the experts.**

Each book features:
Bulleted lists • Call-out boxes • Sample reports • Completely cross-referenced material • Quick-reference graphics with standardization data

---

**I'd like to order the following ESSENTIALS of Psychological Assessment:**

- ❑ WAIS-III Assessment / 28295-2 / $29.95
- ❑ CAS Assessment / 29015-7 / $29.95
- ❑ Millon Inventories Assessment / 29798-4 / $29.95
- ❑ Forensic Psychological Assessment / 33186-4 / $29.95
- ❑ Bayley Scales of Infant Dev II Assessment / 32651-8 / $29.95 / **Oct 99**
- ❑ Myers-Briggs Type Indicator Assessment / 33239-9 / $29.95 / **Nov 99**

**Please send this order form, with your payment (credit card or check) to:**
John Wiley & Sons Publishing, Attn: M. Fellin,
605 Third Avenue, New York, NY 10158

Name _____

Affiliation _____

Address_____

City/State/Zip_____

Phone_____ E-mail_____

Credit Card: ❑ Mastercard ❑ Visa ❑ American Express
(All orders subject to credit approval)

Card Number_____

Exp Date _____

Signature_____

**TO ORDER BY PHONE, CALL 1-800-225-5945**

WILEY

**Essentials of Psychological Assessment Series**
Series Editors, Alan S. Kaufman and Nadeen L. Kaufman

*Essentials of WAIS-III Assessment*
by Alan S. Kaufman and Elizabeth O. Lichtenberger

*Essentials of CAS Assessment*
by Jack A. Naglieri

*Essentials of Millon Inventories Assessment*
by Stephen N. Strack

*Essentials of NEPSY Assessment*
by Sally Kemp, Ursula Kirk, and Marit Korkman

*Essentials of Bayley Scales of Infant Development II Assessment*
by Maureen M. Black and Kathleen Matula

*Essentials of Forensic Psychological Assessment*
by Marc J. Ackerman

*Essentials of MMPI-2 Assessment*
by David S. Nichols

*Essentials of WISC-III and WPPSI-R Assessment*
by Alan S. Kaufman and Elizabeth O. Lichtenberger

# Essentials

## of Myers-Briggs Type Indicator® Assessment

Naomi L. Quenk

John Wiley & Sons, Inc.
NEW YORK • CHICHESTER • WEINHEIM • BRISBANE • SINGAPORE • TORONTO

This book is printed on acid-free paper. ∞

Copyright © 2000 by John Wiley & Sons, Inc. All rights reserved.

Published by John Wiley & Sons, Inc.

Published simultaneously in Canada.

*Myers-Briggs Type Indicator,* MBTI, and *Introduction to Type* are registered trademarks of Consulting Psychologists Press, Inc.

*Strong Interest Inventory* is a registered trademark of Stanford University Press.

This publication is designed to provide accurate and authoritative information in regard to the subject matter covered. It is sold with the understanding that the publisher is not engaged in rendering professional services. If legal, accounting, medical, psychological or any other expert assistance is required, the services of a competent professional person should be sought.

Library of Congress Cataloging-in-Publication Data:

Quenk, Naomi L., 1936–
   Essentials of Myers-Briggs type indicator assessment / Naomi L. Quenk.
      p.  cm. — (Essentials of psychological assessment series)
   Includes bibliographical references and index.
   ISBN 0-471-33239-9 (paper : alk. paper)
      1. Myers-Briggs Type Indicator.  2. Typology (Psychology)
  I. Title.  II. Series.
  BF698.8.M94Q45   1999
  155.2'83—dc21                       99-32552
                                    CIP

Printed in the United States of America.

10  9  8  7  6  5  4  3  2  1

*To Mary McCaulley, friend and mentor*

# CONTENTS

# SERIES PREFACE

In the *Essentials of Psychological Assessment* series, we have attempted to provide the reader with books that will deliver key practical information in the most efficient and accessible style. The series features instruments in a variety of domains, such as cognition, personality, education, and neuropsychology. For the experienced clinician, books in the series will offer a concise yet thorough way to master utilization of the continuously evolving supply of new and revised instruments, as well as a convenient method for keeping up to date on the tried-and-true measures. The novice will find here a prioritized assembly of all the information and techniques that must be at one's fingertips to begin the complicated process of individual psychological diagnosis.

Wherever feasible, visual shortcuts to highlight key points are utilized alongside systematic, step-by-step guidelines. Chapters are focused and succinct. Topics are targeted for an easy understanding of the essentials of administration, scoring, interpretation, and clinical application. Theory and research are continually woven into the fabric of each book, but always to enhance clinical inference, never to sidetrack or overwhelm. We have long been advocates of "intelligent" testing—the notion that a profile of test scores is meaningless unless it is brought to life by the clinical observations and astute detective work of knowledgeable examiners. Test profiles must be used to make a difference in the child's or adult's life, or why bother to test? We want this series to help our readers become the best intelligent testers they can be.

In *Essentials of Myers-Briggs Type Indicator Assessment,* Dr. Naomi Quenk provides expert guidance for clinically applying this most widely used method of assessing healthy personality. Dr. Quenk is coauthor of the 1998 revision of the MBTI manual, which introduces Form M, the revised standard form of the

Myers-Briggs Type Indicator (MBTI®). She is a longtime contributor to theory, research, and clinical understanding of typology and excels in integrating and presenting complex material in a clear and accessible way. Clinicians will find the practical advice and insights for applying the MBTI in the conduct of psychotherapy to be particularly useful.

*Alan S. Kaufman, Ph.D., and Nadeen L. Kaufman, Ed.D., Series Editors*
Yale University School of Medicine

# One

The Myers-Briggs Type Indicator (MBTI) personality inventory is firmly grounded in C. G. Jung's theory of psychological types, first presented in his book *Psychological Types* (1921/1971). MBTI assessment of type has been available in published form since 1956, though its development began some 15 years earlier. A wealth of information has since been generated about the instrument's theoretical basis, its reliability and validity, and its practical application in widely diverse areas. There are three editions of the MBTI manual (Myers, 1962; Myers & McCaulley, 1985; Myers, McCaulley, Quenk, & Hammer, 1998), as well as a comprehensive review of research in seven application areas (Hammer, 1996). These and many other sources contain valuable information about the theory, psychometric characteristics, research relationships, and applications of the MBTI. The sheer magnitude of what is available can be daunting to those new to the instrument as well as to experienced practitioners seeking practical guidance for administering and interpreting the MBTI.

*Essentials of MBTI Assessment* encapsulates the overwhelming amount of MBTI information by providing all key information in a manner that is straightforward and easily accessible. Each chapter includes several "Rapid Reference," "Caution," and "Don't Forget" boxes that highlight important points relevant to each topic. Chapters end with a series of questions designed to solidify what you have read. The primary emphasis is on clinical uses of the MBTI; however, professionals in any area of application will find the basic information they need to effectively administer and interpret the MBTI in their setting.

## HISTORY AND DEVELOPMENT

Jung's *Psychological Types* (1921/1971) was translated into English in 1923. Interest in the work was generally limited to Jungian and psychoanalytic circles in

I

both Europe and America. It was fortuitous, if not remarkable, that two women, Katharine C. Briggs and her daughter, Isabel Briggs Myers (neither of whom had credentials in Jungian analysis or psychological test development), read Jung's work, spent 20 years studying it, and devised an instrument—the MBTI—to assess typology. Their years of intensive reading of Jung and careful observation of individual behavior led to their conclusion that typology could provide a useful way of describing healthy personality differences and, importantly, that such assessment could be put to practical use in people's lives.

Jung's interest in types emerged from his observation of consistent differences among people that were not attributable to their psychopathology. At first he believed that two basic *attitude types*—extraverts and introverts—adequately explained the differences he found. Further observation convinced him that other differences must be at work and that his two-category typology was inadequate. He subsequently added opposite *mental functions* to his descriptive system: two opposite functions of perception, sensation (called Sensing in the MBTI) versus intuition, and two opposite functions of judgment, thinking versus feeling.

Briggs's early interest had been in the variety of ways that people achieved excellence in their lives. Prior to discovering Jung's work, she had studied biographies in an effort to develop her own typology. In addition to opposites similar to those described by Jung, she observed that individuals differed in the way they habitually related to the outside world. Her early observations ultimately led to the addition of a fourth pair of opposites to Jung's system, a Judging versus a Perceiving attitude toward the outer, extraverted world. Although Jung did not explicitly identify this pair of opposites, Briggs and Myers found it to be implicit in his writings.

Published forms of the MBTI have been in existence since 1956. Until 1975, when its publication moved from Educational Testing Service to Consulting Psychologists Press, it was used primarily by a small number of enthusiastic researchers. Consulting Psychologists Press made the MBTI available to all professionals who were qualified to purchase Level B instruments. Since 1975 over 30 million people have taken the Indicator, more than 10 million in the past 5 years. About 2 million people fill out the MBTI annually, making it by far the most widely used instrument for assessing normal personality functioning.

Rapid Reference 1.1 gives a chronological listing of significant events in the history of MBTI development.

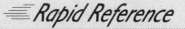
*Rapid Reference*

## 1.1 Background and Development of the MBTI

| | |
|---|---|
| 1917 | Katharine Briggs develops a way of describing individual differences in ways of achieving excellence based on her study of biographies of accomplished individuals. |
| 1923 | Jung's *Psychological Types* is translated into English from the original German, first published in 1921. |
| 1923–1941 | Briggs and Myers study Jung's typology and observe its expression in the behavior of individuals. |
| 1941 | World War II motivates Myers to work on developing an instrument that will give people access to their Jungian type—to capitalize on natural preferences to help the war effort. |
| 1942–1944 | Myers writes and tests items using a small criterion group whose preferences are clear to her. Forms A and B are created. |
| 1942–1956 | MBTI data are collected various samples, including medical and nursing students. |
| 1956 | Educational Testing Service publishes the MBTI as a research instrument. It is available only to researchers. |
| 1956–1962 | Research continues, yielding MBTI Forms C through E. |
| 1962 | The first MBTI manual and MBTI Form F are published by Educational Testing Service. It continues to be classified as a research instrument. |
| 1962–1974 | Researchers at several universities (e.g., University of California at Berkeley and Auburn University) use the MBTI for various research purposes. Mary H. McCaulley, a clinical psychology faculty member at the University of Florida, collaborates with Myers to further test the MBTI, and to create a data bank for storage of MBTI data. |
| 1975 | Consulting Psychologists Press becomes the publisher of MBTI Form F, and makes it available to all professionals qualified to purchase Level B instruments. |
| 1978 | Form G (126 items) replaces Form F (166 items) as the standard form of the MBTI, based on a restandardization of the scales. |
| 1980 | Isabel Briggs Myers dies. |

*continued*

| 1985 | The second edition of the MBTI manual is published, co-authored by Myers and McCaulley. |
| 1987, 1989 | Extended forms of the Indicator, Forms J and K, are published. |
| 1998 | Form M (93 items) replaces Form G as the standard form. It is preceded by extensive exploration of alternative item selection and scoring methods and is standardized on a stratified national sample of the U.S. population. The third edition of the MBTI manual is published. |

A major reason for the popularity of the MBTI is its relevance in many quite diverse areas—education, career development, organizational behavior, group functioning and team development, psychotherapy with individuals and couples, and in multicultural settings. Because of its long history and prevalence as a research instrument, there are well over 4,000 articles listed in an ongoing MBTI bibliography (Center for Applications of Psychological Type, 1999), including more than 1,300 dissertations. The bibliography is updated monthly. The *Journal of Psychological Type* has published 49 volumes primarily devoted to typological research efforts.

*Essentials of MBTI Assessment* focuses on MBTI Form M, the standard form of the instrument that was introduced in 1998. Users who are familiar with Form G, the previous standard form, may be particularly interested in the similarities and differences between the two forms, which are briefly described in Rapid Reference 1.2.

There are two extended forms of the MBTI, Forms J and K, along with associated scoring methods and reports (Mitchell et al., 1999; Quenk & Kummerow, 1997; Saunders, 1987, 1989), which yield additional individualized typological information. The development and uses of these forms, scoring methods, and reports are beyond the scope of this book. Interested readers can find relevant information in the references cited. There is also a type indicator designed for children aged approximately 8 through 14, the Murphy-Meisgeier Type Indicator for Children (Murphy & Meisgeier, 1987), which rests on the same assumptions as the MBTI but contains different items, scoring method, and guidelines for interpretation.

≣ *Rapid Reference*

### 1.2 Similarities and Differences Between Form M and Form G

**Similarities**

- Both use forced-choice items to elicit preference.
- Both encompass the four dichotomies specified in the Jung/Myers theory.
- Items on both are worded in neutral and positive ways.
- More than half (51 items) are the same on both forms.

**Differences**

- Item response theory was used both to select Form M items and to score the instrument. Item response theory provides greater precision of measurement, especially around the midpoint of each dichotomy; Form G used Myers's prediction ratio method.
- There are 42 new items with updated wording.
- There is one less item scored for type (93 rather than Form G's 94 items).
- There are no different scoring weights for males and females on the T–F scale, as there were for Form G.
- Item weights are based on a new national sample of adult respondents.

## THEORETICAL FOUNDATION OF THE MBTI

The Jung/Myers theory of psychological types is a way of describing and explaining certain consistent differences in the ways that normal people use their minds. The MBTI purports to identify these differences through a 93-item, self-administered, paper-and-pencil questionnaire. Results show the respondent's preferences on each of four pairs of opposite categories, which are called dichotomies. According to the theory, all eight categories, or preference poles, included in the MBTI are used at least some of the time by every person. However, individuals have an innate disposition toward one category (pole) of each dichotomy. The goal of MBTI assessment is to accurately identify preferences by sorting respondents into the categories to which they are already disposed. To elicit preferences between categorical poles rather than the degree of liking for or use of each opposite pole, all items are presented in a forced-choice format. This question format requires the respondent to choose between two mental functions or two attitudes in order to identify which is naturally preferred. If respondents were instead asked to indicate their use of or liking for each pole separately (as with a Likert-type rating scale), preference for one over the other could not be readily distinguished. Forcing respondents to choose between two legitimate ways of using their minds most directly and clearly elicits a preference.

The mental functions and attitudes that are the basic elements of the Jung/Myers theory follow.

## The Opposite Functions of Perception: Sensing and Intuition

Sensing perception uses the five senses to become aware of facts and details occurring in the present. When Sensing perception is being used, the perceiver is grounded in and trusting of the evidence of the senses, focusing on concrete reality, and the gathering of facts and details. There is trust in what is known and can be verified. With little conscious effort, a person who prefers Sensing has a memory that is specific, detailed, literal, and complete. Without exercising considerable conscious effort, he or she is less likely to give credence and be interested in hypotheses, the unknown, and future possibilities. Sensing is a process that avoids inferences and conjecture and prefers instead to make decisions based on verifiable facts. People who prefer Sensing can experience any requirement to speculate on an unknown future as a pointless distraction from what is important.

Intuitive perception looks at patterns, meanings, and future possibilities that are believed to be implicit in current reality. When Intuition is being used, the perceiver focuses on concepts, ideas, and theories, inferring connections among diverse pieces of information. With little conscious effort, Intuitive perception moves quickly and easily from what is present in the here and now to what is implied and possible in the future. Without exercising considerable conscious effort, a person who prefers Intuition has difficulty memorizing and using facts without putting them into an interesting context. Intuition is a process that is less experienced and interested in acquiring, remembering, and using facts and details for their own sake. People who prefer Intuition can experience such a focus as inhibiting to their free flow of ideas and as a pointless distraction from what is important.

## The Opposite Functions of Judgment: Thinking and Feeling

Thinking judgment applies specific criteria and principles in a linear, logical analysis of Sensing or Intuitive information. The goal is to arrive at the objective truth or a reasonable approximation of truth. When Thinking judgment is being used, the person making the judgment takes an objective and dispassionate approach to the available data. With little conscious effort, individuals who prefer Thinking can maintain an objective stance and personal distance by keeping issues of their own and others' personal values and well-being separate from their decision making. Typically, only after a Thinking conclusion has been arrived at can conscious effort be devoted to considering issues of welfare and harmony.

Feeling judgment applies specific, usually personally held values to assess the relative importance of the Sensing or Intuitive information available. When Feeling judgment is being used, there is concern for the impacts and consequences of a decision on individuals or groups of people. The goal of a Feeling decision is to maximize harmony and well-being for people and situations. Without conscious effort, people who prefer Feeling take into account their own and others' feelings, values, and welfare. They use personal connections and empathy with the people affected by a decision to arrive at a conclusion. People who prefer Feeling can readily recognize logical principles and objective criteria for decision making. However, without exercising considerable conscious effort, they avoid using such criteria if harm and disharmony will result.

The terms chosen by Jung and retained by Myers for these two opposites have some unfortunate potential "surplus meanings." Therefore it is important to recognize that in the MBTI Thinking judgment does imply the absence of emotion but rather an automatic setting aside of value considerations for the sake of impartiality and objectivity. Feeling judgment does not refer to the experience and expression of emotion. Emotion is separate from Feeling judgment in that emotion is accompanied by a physiological response that is independent of decision making. Thinking types and Feeling types can be equally passionate about a favored position in spite of contradictory evidence that violates certain logical principles (for Thinking types) or certain values (for Feeling types). Similarly, a Thinking judgment is not more intelligent or correct than a Feeling judgment. In the Jung/Myers theory, Thinking and Feeling describe rational processes that follow laws of reason; that is, they evaluate data using definite criteria—logical principles for Thinking and personal values for Feeling.

## The Opposite Attitudes of Energy: Extraversion and Introversion

Extraversion as an attitude directs psychic energy to and receives energy from the outer world of people, things, and action. When in the Extraverted attitude, a person interacts with the environment, receives energy through actively engaging with people and activities, and takes a trial-and-error approach to acquiring new experiences and skills. People who prefer Extraversion tend to think most effectively when interacting and talking to others and it takes little conscious effort for them to approach others and explore the outer world. Without conscious effort, it is hard for them to think only internally, since they often become aware of what they are thinking only when they are verbalizing. Spending too much time without external activity can result in fatigue and low motivation.

Introversion as an attitude directs psychic energy to the inner world of ideas, reflection, and internal experiences and is energized by operating in that realm. When in the Introverted attitude, a person spends time reflecting on and reviewing ideas and experiences, and observes and thinks about whether or not to interact with new people or try new outside activities. People who prefer Introversion tend to think internally before expressing their thoughts to others. It takes little conscious effort to keep what they are thinking to themselves. Without conscious effort, it is uncomfortable and difficult for them to express their thoughts without first reflecting on them. Spending too little time alone and too much time interacting with people and the environment can result in fatigue and low motivation.

## The Two Opposite Attitudes Toward the Outside World: Judging and Perceiving

A Judging attitude involves the habitual use of one of the judging functions, Thinking or Feeling, when interacting with the outer world. When a Judging attitude is being used, there is a desire to reach a conclusion (use judgment) and make a decision as quickly and efficiently as possible. Without conscious effort, individuals who prefer a Judging attitude are organized, structured, effectively work within schedules, and begin tasks sufficiently early so that deadlines can be comfortably met. Without exercising considerable conscious effort, they resist putting off decision making, working without a set plan, and operating in an environment where there are frequent interruptions and diversions.

A Perceiving attitude involves the habitual use of one of the perceiving functions, Sensing or Intuition, when interacting with the outer world. When a Perceiving attitude is being used, there is a desire to collect as much information (i.e., perceive) as possible before coming to a conclusion. Without conscious effort, a person who prefers a Perceiving attitude is flexible, adaptable, and spontaneous when operating in the outside world, works comfortably and effectively when there is pressure of an imminent deadline, and welcomes interruptions and diversions because they stimulate new energy and may provide additional useful information. Without considerable conscious effort, it is difficult for him or her to start on tasks very far in advance of a deadline, operate within set schedules, and be orderly and methodical in pursuing desired goals.

A frequent source of misunderstanding for people with regard to the Judging and Perceiving attitude is knowing that these attitudes describe ways of relating to the outside, extraverted world *regardless of one's preference for Extraversion or Introversion.* People who prefer a Judging attitude behave in a Judging manner while extraverting (extraverting either Thinking or Feeling, whichever they prefer); people who prefer a Perceiving attitude behave in a Perceiving manner while extraverting (extraverting either Sensing or Intuition, whichever they prefer).

Rapid Reference 1.3 summarizes the four dichotomies that constitute a four-letter type and indicates their designation as either attitudes or functions. The order of presenting the dichotomies in this Rapid Reference is the one typically used when presenting type to clients, rather than the one used in the preceding discussion. It also corresponds to the order used in the standard type code. Alternative strategies for presenting the functions and attitudes are considered in Chapter 4. Like all definitions and descriptions of MBTI preferences and types, the brief definitions presented here are designed to be neutral and positive in tone, conveying that neither pole of any dichotomy is favored over its opposite.

## 1.3 The Four Dichotomies of the MBTI

### The Extraversion–Introversion Dichotomy
### (attitudes or orientations of energy)

Extraversion (E)

Directing energy mainly toward the outer world of people and objects

Introversion (I)

Directing energy mainly toward the inner world of experiences and ideas

### The Sensing–Intuition Dichotomy
### (functions or processes of perception)

Sensing (S)

Focusing mainly on what can be perceived by the five senses

Intuition (N)

Focusing mainly on perceiving patterns and interrelationships

### The Thinking–Feeling Dichotomy
### (functions or processes of judgment)

Thinking (T)

Basing conclusions on logical analysis with a focus on objectivity and detachment

Feeling (F)

Basing conclusions on personal or social values with a focus on understanding and harmony

### The Judging–Perceiving Dichotomy
### (attitudes or orientations to the outer world)

Judging (J)

Preferring the decisiveness and closure that results from dealing with the outer world using one of the judging processes (T or F)

Perceiving (P)

Preferring the flexibility and spontaneity that results from dealing with the outer world using one of the perceiving processes (S or N)

An individual's preferences can be summarized in a four-letter code, each letter standing for one of the eight preferences, such as ISTJ for Introverted, Sensing, Thinking, Judging or ENFP for Extraverted, Intuitive, Feeling, Perceiving. All possible combinations of preferences yield 16 different types. All 16 types are seen as valid and legitimate ways of being psychologically healthy, adapted, and successful, though their interests, talents, and general outlooks are likely to be quite different.

## Dynamic Personality Type

Personality type is the result of the interplay of a person's four preferences, represented by one pole of each dichotomy. This interplay is of a dynamic and interactive nature rather than a static or additive one: The whole type is hypothesized to be greater than the sum of the four preferences it encompasses. It is assumed that every individual has access to all eight preference poles—Extraversion *and* Introversion, Sensing *and* Intuition, Thinking *and* Feeling, a Judging attitude *and* a Perceiving attitude. The underlying rationale for this assumption is that each of these functions and attitudes is necessary for psychological adaptation and therefore is present in every person's psychological makeup. However, each is likely to be used with greater or lesser comfort and facility by an individual, depending on its dynamic status within his or her type.

Dynamic status is represented in the Jung/Myers theory as the likely use and development of the system's four functions, or processes (Sensing, Intuition, Thinking, Feeling), which may be dominant (most used, capable of development, and under conscious control), auxiliary (second in use, development, and conscious access), tertiary (third in use and development, and relatively unconscious), or inferior (least used and developed, and primarily unconscious). The theory also specifies that the auxiliary function must be the "other kind" of mental function to that of the dominant; that is, if the dominant function is one of the perceiving functions (Sensing or Intuition), then the auxiliary function must be one of the judging functions (Thinking or Feeling); if the dominant function is one of the judging functions (Thinking or Feeling), then the auxiliary function must be one of the perceiving functions

(Sensing or Intuition). By conceptualizing the psyche in this way, an individual has reasonable conscious access to one kind of perception and one kind of judgment so that two critical human endeavors can be directed and controlled.

Both Jung and Myers specified that people who by nature prefer the Extraverted attitude and are most comfortable in that attitude, tend to use their dominant, most consciously accessible function when extraverting; people who by nature prefer the Introverted attitude and are most comfortable in that attitude, tend to use their dominant, most consciously accessible function when introverting. Jung, with Myers and Briggs concurring, were also clear that the fourth, inferior function, operated primarily in the opposite, less preferred attitude of Extraversion or Introversion. It should be noted that Jung's use of the term *inferior function* was in contrast to his alternative term for the dominant function, which was the *superior function*. The fourth function is "inferior" only in the sense of being last in its accessibility to conscious control.

Jung did not provide clear guidelines regarding the attitude of the auxiliary and tertiary functions. Myers and Briggs amplified and extended Jung's theory by specifying that for sound and healthy adaptation, the auxiliary function operated in the less preferred attitude. In extending Jung's system in this way, they provided for a comfortable and effective way of extraverting and introverting, both of which are necessary for human functioning.

With regard to the attitude of the tertiary function, Myers and Briggs assumed it was opposite to that of the dominant function, as were the auxiliary and inferior functions. This convention was followed in all three MBTI manuals, although there are alternative views regarding the issue. Because there is relatively little theoretical or empirical evidence favoring one attitude or the other as habitual for the tertiary function, an attitude is not specified in this book.

The assumptions of a hierarchy and habitual attitudinal direction are reflected in the designation of each type, for example, Introverted Intuition with Extraverted Thinking. The first term identifies the type's dominant function and attitude whereas the second term specifies the auxiliary function and attitude. The tertiary and inferior functions do not appear in the type code or title of the type, but they are implicit opposites: The tertiary is opposite to the auxiliary in function, and the inferior is opposite to the dominant in both function and attitude.

The hierarchy of functions and associated attitudes is also implicit in the type description of the four-letter type in question. The type description is a detailed narrative that is the primary way that type results are presented. The most theoretically grounded type descriptions (Myers, 1998; Myers et al., 1998) are an orderly presentation of the personality qualities that result from having a dominant function operating in the preferred attitude, an auxiliary function in the less preferred attitude, a tertiary function that is relatively unconscious, and an inferior function that takes the less preferred attitude and is largely unconscious.

## Rationale for Determining Type Dynamics

The method for determining type dynamics can seem confusing to people new to type, but it is actually straightforward once the basic assumptions detailed earlier are recognized. The following points reinforce the theoretical assumptions underlying the method:

- If the dominant (first) function is one of the Perceiving pair (Sensing or Intuition), the auxiliary (second) will be one of the Judging pair (Thinking or Feeling), and vice versa.
- The dominant function tends to be used in the preferred attitude of Extraversion or Introversion, thus stipulating that the favorite mental activity operates with the preferred kind of energy.
- The auxiliary function is complementary to the dominant function and tends to be used in the less preferred attitude of Extraversion or Introversion, thus giving a person access to both the other important kind of mental activity (judgment or perception, depending on which is the dominant function) and to the less preferred kind of energy (Extraversion or Introversion, whichever is less preferred). Remember that both perception and judgment are necessary for adaptation—as are both kinds of energy.
- The tertiary function is opposite to the auxiliary. An attitude for the tertiary function is not designated due to differences of opinion in this regard.
- The inferior, fourth function is opposite to the dominant function in both function and attitude (e.g., if the dominant function is Extraverted Thinking, the inferior function is Introverted Feeling).

Recall that the J–P dichotomy identifies which function the type uses in the Extraverted attitude—regardless of whether or not Extraversion is the preferred attitude: A person with a Judging (J) preference extraverts either Thinking or Feeling, whichever of the two is preferred; a person with a Perceiving (P) preference extraverts Sensing or Intuition, whichever one of the two is preferred. Because the Jung/Myers theory specifies the use of the dominant function in the preferred attitude and the auxiliary in the less preferred, it follows that (a) for extraverts the function that is extraverted is the dominant function, and the function that is introverted is the auxiliary function; and (b) for introverts the function that is extraverted is the auxiliary function, because their dominant function is used in their preferred attitude of Introversion.

**Rules to Determine Type Dynamics**

The assumptions of type dynamics lead to a logical procedure for determining the dynamics of any four-letter type. Remember that the first letter of the code shows the energy preference, the second letter the perception preference, the third letter the judgment preference, and the fourth letter the preference for using judgment or perception while extraverting. We will illustrate the procedure using two types who differ only in their J or P preference, INFJ and INFP:

Rule 1. One of the two middle letters is the dominant function; the other is the auxiliary function. *Example:* For both INFJ and INFP, N or F is dominant; N or F is auxiliary.

Rule 2. One of the two middle letters is extraverted; the other is introverted. *Example:* For both INFJ and INFP, N or F is extraverted; N or F is introverted.

Rule 3. The last letter (J or P) always tells us which of the two middle letters is extraverted. If the last letter is J, Thinking (T) or Feeling (F) is extraverted because Thinking and Feeling are the two judging functions. *Example:* For INFJ, F is extraverted, and applying Rule 2, N is introverted (i.e., $N_i F_e$).

If the last letter is P, Sensing (S) or Intuition (N) is extraverted because Sensing and Intuition are the two perceiving functions. *Example:* For INFP, N is extraverted, and applying Rule 2, F is introverted (i.e., $N_e F_i$).

Rule 4. The first letter tells us what the preferred attitude is, either Extraversion (E) or Introversion (I). *Example:* For INFJ, the preferred attitude is Introversion (I) (i.e., I $N_i F_e$ J). For INFP, the preferred attitude is Introversion (I) (i.e., I $N_e F_i$ P).

Rule 5. The dominant function is typically used in the preferred attitude of Extraversion or Introversion. *Example:* For I$N_i F_e$J, the middle letter that is introverted is N for Intuition. The dominant function of INFJ is therefore Introverted Intuition ($N_i$). For I$N_e F_i$P, the middle letter that is introverted is F for Feeling. The dominant function of INFP is therefore Introverted Feeling ($F_i$).

Rule 6. Following Rule 1, the "other letter" (the one that identifies the auxiliary function) for I$N_i F_e$J is Feeling, which, according to Rule 2, is extraverted. *Example:* The auxiliary function for INFJ is Extraverted Feeling. The dynamics of INFJ are stated as *dominant introverted Intuition with auxiliary extraverted Feeling.* The "other letter" (the auxiliary function) for I$N_e F_i$P is Intuition, which, according to Rule 2, is extraverted. The auxiliary function for INFP is extraverted Intuition. The dynamics of INFP are stated as *dominant introverted Feeling with auxiliary extraverted Intuition.*

Rule 7. The tertiary function is opposite to the auxiliary function. We won't specify an attitude for the tertiary function. *Example:* For INFJ, Thinking (T) is the opposite of auxiliary F and is the tertiary function (i.e., $I\,{}^{N_i\,F_e}_{\;\;\;\;T}\,J$). For INFP, Sensing (S) is the opposite of auxiliary N and is the tertiary function (i.e., $I\,{}^{N_e\,F_i}_{\;\;S}\,P$).

Rule 8. The inferior function is opposite to the dominant function and takes the opposite attitude. *Example:* For I$N_i F_e$J, Extraverted Sensing is the opposite of dominant introverted Intuition and is therefore the inferior function (i.e., $I\,{}^{N_i}_{S_e}\,{}^{F_e}\,J$). For I$N_e F_i$P, Extraverted Thinking is the opposite of dominant introverted Feeling and is therefore the inferior function (i.e., $I\,{}^{N_e}\,{}^{F_i}_{T_e}\,P$).

Note that INFJ and INFP have three type preferences in common, I, N, and F, so we might reasonably expect that these two types are very much the same. But according to type theory, their dynamics—the nature and direction of flow of energy of their mental functions—are quite different. These differences show up in the behavior of these two types and are in accord with these types' dynamic differences. This important information can be put to practical use in the assessment of their personalities and functioning during the course of counseling and psychotherapy.

To further illuminate the effects of type dynamics, let's contrast the type ENFP with INFP, two types that also have three letters in common. Will these two types be as different in dynamics as the INFJ and INFP? Briefly, ENFP extraverts the preferred perceiving function, N. Since Extraversion is the preferred attitude, $N_e$ (Extraverted Intuition) is the dominant function. ENFP introverts the preferred judging function, F. Since Introversion is the less preferred attitude, $F_i$ (Introverted Feeling) is the auxiliary function. The tertiary function is opposite to the auxiliary, and is therefore T. The inferior function is opposite in function and attitude to the dominant function, and is therefore $S_i$ (Introverted Sensing). The total dynamics for ENFP are $^E N_e F_i^{\ P.}_{S_i T}$. The total dynamics for INFP are $^I N_e F_i^{\ P.}_{S\ T_e}$.

In an important way, INFP and ENFP could be considered more similar to each other than INFP and INFJ because they use their two conscious functions, the dominant and auxiliary *in the same attitudes.* Yet their more unconscious expressions can be expected to be rather different, because for ENFP, Introverted Sensing is the inferior function and Thinking is the tertiary function, whereas for INFP, Extraverted Thinking is the inferior function and Sensing is the tertiary function. This and the differential availability of energy for their respective functions account for some important observable differences between these two types.

Similar differences occur for other types who share middle letters but differ on either J and P, or E and I—or both. Chapter 4 discusses some of the dynamic differences between types, and Chapter 6 includes examples of their effects in relation to clinical applications of the MBTI.

You can test your understanding of type dynamics by following the steps in Don't Forget 1.1 (page 18), which focuses on two other types that differ only in their preference for E or I, ESTP and ISTP. You can also figure out the dynamics of any other type and check your accuracy by consulting Rapid Reference 1.4, which shows each four-letter type, its dynamic designation, and its specified tertiary and inferior function.

## *Rapid Reference*

### 1.4 Dynamic Characteristics of the 16 Types

| Type | Dynamic Name | Tertiary | Inferior |
|------|--------------|----------|----------|
| **ISTJ** | Introverted Sensing with Extraverted Thinking | Feeling | Extraverted Intuition |
| **ISFJ** | Introverted Sensing with Extraverted Feeling | Thinking | Extraverted Intuition |
| **ESTP** | Extraverted Sensing with Introverted Thinking | Feeling | Introverted Intuition |
| **ESFP** | Extraverted Sensing with Introverted Feeling | Thinking | Introverted Intuition |
| **INTJ** | Introverted Intuition with Extraverted Thinking | Feeling | Extraverted Sensing |
| **INFJ** | Introverted Intuition with Extraverted Feeling | Thinking | Extraverted Sensing |
| **ENTP** | Extraverted Intuition with Introverted Thinking | Feeling | Introverted Sensing |
| **ENFP** | Extraverted Intuition with Introverted Feeling | Thinking | Introverted Sensing |
| **ISTP** | Introverted Thinking with Extraverted Sensing | Intuition | Extraverted Feeling |
| **INTP** | Introverted Thinking with Extraverted Intuition | Sensing | Extraverted Feeling |
| **ESTJ** | Extraverted Thinking with Introverted Sensing | Intuition | Introverted Feeling |
| **ENTJ** | Extraverted Thinking with Introverted Intuition | Sensing | Introverted Feeling |
| **ISFP** | Introverted Feeling with Extraverted Sensing | Intuition | Extraverted Thinking |
| **INFP** | Introverted Feeling with Extraverted Intuition | Sensing | Extraverted Thinking |
| **ESFJ** | Extraverted Feeling with Introverted Sensing | Intuition | Introverted Thinking |
| **ENFJ** | Extraverted Feeling with Introverted Intuition | Sensing | Introverted Thinking |

# DON'T FORGET

## 1.1 Finding the Dynamics for ESTP and ISTP

|  | ESTP | ISTP |
|---|---|---|
| Rule 1: The dominant function is either: | S or T | S or T |
| The auxiliary function is either: | S or T | S or T |
| Rule 2. The function that is extraverted is either: | S or T | S or T |
| The function that is introverted is either: | S or T | S or T |
| Rule 3: The last letter is: | P | P |
| So the extraverted function is: | $S_e$ | $S_e$ |
| *Applying Rule 2, the introverted function is:* | $T_i$ | $T_i$ |
| Rule 4. The preferred attitude is: | E | I |
| Rule 5. The function that is used in the preferred attitude is: | $S_e$ | $T_i$ |
| The dominant function is therefore: | $S_e$ | $T_i$ |
| Rule 6. The function used is the less preferred attitude is: | $T_i$ | $S_e$ |
| The auxiliary function is therefore: | $T_i$ | $S_e$ |
| Rule 7. The function opposite the auxiliary function is: | F | N |
| The tertiary function is therefore: | F | N |
| Rule 8. The function/attitude opposite the dominant function is: | $N_i$ | $F_e$ |
| The inferior function is therefore: | $N_i$ | $F_e$ |

## A Fundamental Theoretical Distinction

The chief advantage of a theoretically based assessment device is that it provides a cohesive structure within which personality differences can be described, explained, and predicted. However, this puts extra construction and validation requirements on the developer and an added burden on the user, who must understand the theory well enough to apply the instrument appropriately. A fundamental feature of Jung's theory—and therefore the construction and accurate interpretation of the MBTI—is that it postulates qualitatively distinct *categories* rather than more familiar behavioral *traits* that vary along a continuum.

Don't Forget 1.2 shows the differences between MBTI type assessment and contrasting trait approaches. Caution 1.1 (page 20) lists the dangers of

# DON'T FORGET

................................................................................................

## 1.2 Differences Between Trait-Based Assessment and MBTI Assessment

| Trait Assessments | MBTI Assessment |
|---|---|
| Assume universal qualities—people vary only in the amount of the trait possessed | Assumes qualitatively distinct categories—individuals prefer one or the other category |
| Measure the amount of each trait | Sorts individuals into one or the other category |
| Scores are expected to be normally distributed—most scores are in the middle | Scores are expected to be bimodal—few scores at the midpoint |
| Scores are variables that show how much of the trait a person has | Scores are estimates of confidence in the accuracy of the sorting procedure—placement into the category indicated |
| Interpretive interest is in people at the extremes of the distribution | Interpretive interest is in people near the midpoint, where accuracy of sorting may be in doubt |
| Assume that behavior is caused by relevant underlying traits | Assumes that behavior is an expression of underlying type preferences |
| Assume that traits are largely independent of each other | Assumes that the four type preferences interact dynamically to form a whole that is different from the sum of its parts |
| Traits are usually identified by a single descriptor | Type dichotomies are identified by their two opposite poles |
| Very high and/or very low scores on a trait can be negative or diagnostic | The numerical portion of MBTI results has no negative or diagnostic meaning |

# CAUTION

## 1.1 Consequences of Mistaking Type Categories for Trait Variables

- Reading positive or negative meaning into numerical preference clarity indexes—that either more clarity, less clarity, or moderate clarity is better or worse
- Assuming that people with very clear preferences have "more of" the function or attitude than people with less clear preferences
- Believing that greater clarity implies greater skill or maturity of use of a preference
- Inferring that one or the other preference pole of a dichotomy is "better" or "healthier" than the other
- Assessing people from the standpoint of a single norm of psychological health rather than considering what is usual and expected for their type

misinterpreting type categories as trait variables. Avoiding these errors is essential for accurate administration (Chapter 2) and interpretation (Chapter 4) of the instrument.

## RESEARCH FOUNDATION

Throughout its long history, the MBTI has undergone continuous and meticulous research—on its construction, the various ways of estimating its reliability, and the abundant and varied studies regarding its validity in diverse areas of interest.

### Construction of Items and Scales

Theoretical requirements were primary in the development of items and construction of the four MBTI scales. Items ask about simple surface behaviors and attitudes that are designed to reflect the presence of an underlying preference for one or the other mental function (S or N; T or F) or attitude (E or I; J or P). Because the goal was to identify slight as well as clear preferences on each dichotomy, items were not worded extremely. Because using logically opposed wording on some items could engender adverse social desirability (e.g., "convincing" versus "unconvincing"), opposite choices were designed as "psychological equivalents" that would be meaningful to people holding the preference in question (e.g., "convincing" versus "touching"). The major concern in scale construction was to achieve maximum accuracy in the placement of the midpoint separating the poles of each dichotomy, since the goal was to sort people into categories rather than measure the amount of a trait. As will be seen in Chapters 2, 3, and 4, item wording and scale construction have an impact on administration, scoring, and interpretation of the MBTI, and they are discussed further in those contexts.

## Norms

Norms are appropriate for trait measures but inappropriate in a type-based instrument. Norms are therefore not reported for the MBTI. Instead, type tables are typically used to report the frequency and percent of each of the 16 types in a sample of interest. To draw meaningful conclusions about the frequency of the types in a particular sample, an appropriate base population is used for comparison. For example, if one wishes to know which types, if any, are over- or underrepresented among Ph.D. psychologists, the comparison base population would be holders of the Ph.D. degree in a wide range of disciplines; if interest was in the types of college students who are likely to seek personal counseling, the appropriate base population would be a general sample of college students. The statistic used to show over- and underrepresentation of types is called a self-selection ratio (SSR), and type tables that show SSR data are called selection ratio type tables (McCaulley, 1985). The SSR, also referred to as the Index of Attraction, is calculated by dividing the percentage of a type in the sample of interest by the percentage of that type in the base population to obtain a ratio. Ratios greater than 1.00 indicate overrepresentation of the type relative to the base population, ratios of less than 1.00 show underrepresentation of the type, and ratios around 1.00 reflect about the same representation as the base population. The statistical significance of SSRs is estimated using a chi-square technique. For example, research on educationally oriented leisure activities for each of the 16 types (DiTiberio, 1998) reported an SSR of 2.64 ($p < .01$) for INFJs for the category Writing, and an SSR of 0.45 ($p < .05$) for this same type for the category Watching Sporting Events; ISTJs showed an SSR of 1.21 ($p < .01$) for Watching Sporting Events and an SSR of 0.52 ($p < .01$) for Writing. Thus a leisure activity that is quite attractive to INFJs is significantly unattractive to ISTJs, and one that significantly attracts ISTJs is significantly unattractive to INFJs. (See Appendix A for an example of a Selection Ratio Type Table for a large sample of counselors.)

## Reliability

Internal consistency and test-retest reliability have been reported for each scale of the MBTI and vary somewhat depending on the nature of the sample studied. Coefficient alpha results available for the largest and most general sample of male and female adults ($N = 2,859$) tested with Form M are .91 for the E–I and T–F scales and .92 for the S–N and J–P scales (Myers et al., 1998). Test-retest reliabilities are given for each scale separately and for whole four-letter types. Because type is hypothesized to remain stable over the life span, this latter measure of reliability is the most important. Test-retest reliabilities vary somewhat with the interval between administrations and also with the age of sample members; younger samples tend to have somewhat lower reliabilities, a result in accord with the theory, which hypothesizes that type develops over the life span and is more likely to be incompletely developed in younger individuals. The developmental hypothesis and its empirical verification are relevant to both administration and especially interpretation of type to clients in different ages and stages of life. With a 4-week interval between administrations, using the most general sample available ($N = 258$), 66% reported all four letters the same and 91% were the same on three out of four preferences. Detailed information on these estimates and additional reliability information can be found in the most recent MBTI manual (Myers et al., 1998).

## Validity

A theory-based test must demonstrate that it adequately reflects the theory it purports to represent. For the MBTI, this entails demonstrating that the preference poles of each dichotomy correspond to Jung/Myers definitions and, most important, that the dynamic interactions hypothesized by Jung and Myers occur. Years of correlational and behavioral research demonstrate the correspondence of the eight preference poles to theoretical prediction (Hammer, 1996; Myers & McCaulley, 1985). More recently, several different forms of evidence supporting the dynamic hypothesis have been reported (Myers et al., 1998).

A variety of statistical methods have been utilized in MBTI research, including the SSR method described earlier. Correlational research looks at one dichotomy at a time and treats MBTI data as though they varied along a continuum, a method that contradicts the MBTI assumption of qualitatively distinct categories. These and other studies of individual dichotomies do not address the dynamic aspect of the MBTI, although they can provide useful information for practitioners about some of the behavioral traits that develop as a result of the exercise of underlying type preferences. The most fruitful lines of research look at the behavior of whole types and dynamic qualities of those types. Chapter 6 applies some of the results of studies of whole types and type dynamics to clinical issues.

## COMPREHENSIVE REFERENCES

*MBTI Manual: A Guide to the Development and Use of the Myers-Briggs Type Indicator* (Myers et al., 1998) provides the most complete and detailed theoretical, psychometric, and research information on the MBTI, as well as practical guidance for its use in five areas of application.

*MBTI Applications: A Decade of Research on the Myers-Briggs Type Indicator* (Hammer, 1996) contains contributed chapters summarizing the reliability and validity of the MBTI as well as research that was completed in the decade after publication of the 1985 MBTI manual.

*CAPT Bibliography for the Myers-Briggs Type Indicator* is a frequently updated bibliography of published and unpublished work on the MBTI. It is available in printed form and on disk from the Center for Applications of Psychological Type. A library of type resources is housed in the same location.

The *Journal of Psychological Type* is published quarterly and is devoted entirely to research and application articles and reviews on psychological type. The journal was first published in 1978 as an annual. Rapid Reference 1.5 provides basic information on the MBTI and its publisher.

# *Rapid Reference*

......................................................................................

## 1.5 The Myers-Briggs Type Indicator Standard Form M

**Author:** Isabel Briggs Myers and Katharine C. Briggs

**Publication date:** 1998

**What the instrument provides:** Identification of Jungian personality type

**Age range:** Approximately 12 years and up

**Administration time:** 15–25 minutes

**Qualifications of examiners:** Undergraduate or graduate course in psychological tests and measurement *or* successful completion of an MBTI Qualifying Training Program sanctioned by the publisher

**Publisher:** Consulting Psychologists Press
3803 East Bayshore Rd.
Palo Alto, CA 94303
Ordering phone number: 800-624-1765
Web site: www.mbti.com

**Comprehensive bibliography:**
Center for Applications of Psychological Type
2815 NW 13th St., Suite 401
Gainesville, FL 32609
Phone: 800-777-CAPT

## 🖋 TEST YOURSELF 🖋

1. **Why are forced-choice questions appropriate for the MBTI and a Likert-type scale inappropriate?**

2. **What are three consequences of treating type preferences as though they were behavioral traits?**

3. **Why are both poles of a dichotomy described in neutral or positive ways?**

    (a) to promote self-esteem in self-critical people

    (b) to communicate the legitimacy of opposite ways of being

    (c) so that people will be motivated to identify their preference

    (d) both b and c

4. **MBTI Form M uses the same item-selection criteria and scoring method as did previous forms of the Indicator.** True or False?

5. **What was Myers and Briggs's main purpose in developing the MBTI?**

    (a) to make typology useful in people's lives

    (b) to counteract the negative influence of trait theories

    (c) to encourage Jungian analysts to take an empirical rather than anecdotal approach in working with patients

    (d) none of the above

6. **Which of the following sets of dichotomies are termed "attitudes"?**

    (a) E–I and T–F

    (b) E–I and S–N

    (c) E–I and J–P

    (d) S–N and J–P

7. **According to type theory, type preferences are**

    (a) habits that are learned through interacting with the environment.

    (b) innate dispositions that develop over time.

    (c) more clear in young people than in mature adults.

    (d) likely to change at midlife.

*continued*

8. **What is the self-selection ratio useful for?**
   (a) comparing trait approaches and type approaches to personality
   (b) determining which types will be successful in different careers
   (c) showing whether some types select and other types avoid a particular career
   (d) all of the above

9. **Why are correlational studies of the MBTI limited?**
   (a) They can only look at one scale at a time.
   (b) They violate the assumption of dichotomies.
   (c) They cannot test the dynamic aspect of the instrument.
   (d) all of the above

10. **When respondents read item choices on the MBTI, why might they be likely to say, "But I do both of those!"?**

11. **What do type preferences reflect?**
   (a) what you are able to do under pressure
   (b) what you are comfortable doing under pressure
   (c) what feels natural and comfortable when there is no pressure
   (d) all of the above

12. **Why is the wording of some MBTI items not logically opposite?**

13. **What was the E–I dichotomy of the MBTI was designed to do?**
   (a) measure how extraverted or introverted a person is
   (b) determine whether a person has a preference for Extraversion or Introversion
   (c) both a and b
   (d) neither a nor b

14. **The dominant function for ENFP is**
   (a) Extraverted Feeling.
   (b) Extraverted Perceiving.
   (c) Extraverted Intuition.
   (d) Introverted Intuition.

**15. Type theory postulates that everyone uses each mental function and attitude at least some of the time.** True or False?

*Answers:* 1. Likert scales elicit *degree of* rather than the required *preference for*; 2. Seeing one pole as "healthier" than the other; thinking the preference clarity index indicates "how much preference" a person has; defining one pole as a deficit in the other; 3. d; 4. b; 5. a; 6. c; 7. b; 8. c; 9. d; 10. Both poles are adaptive, and people therefore use both some of the time; 11. c; 12. Logical opposites can yield socially undesirable choices, so *psychological* rather than logical equivalence is used; 13. b; 14. c; 15. a

## Two

## HOW TO ADMINISTER THE MBTI

The Myers-Briggs Type Indicator personality inventory is essentially self-administered, and the question and answer booklets contain the basic instructions needed for filling out the questionnaire. There are a number of administration issues, however, that can have an impact on obtaining valid MBTI results. For example, respondents can purposely answer items so as to appear to be a particular kind of person, rather than answering according to their actual inclinations. The instrument itself does not include any way of detecting such possible response distortion. Respondents should therefore be provided with good reasons to be candid in their answers and given little reason to misrepresent themselves. Supplying the right kind and amount of information before administration generally maximizes valid results. The relevant administration guidelines are directly or indirectly related to type theory as it was described in Chapter 1.

### HOW TO INTRODUCE THE MBTI

Providing clients with an appropriate test-taking attitude is essential. Type theory assumes that both poles of each dichotomy are used by every individual, though typically with different frequency, confidence, enthusiasm, and ease. MBTI items therefore ask the respondent to choose between two options that are familiar and acceptable. The respondent is asked to choose the option that is most natural, comfortable, and automatic—what he or she does when not under the pressure of a time limit or an external reward or coercion. However, situational demands can sometimes blur or mask natural preference, leading certain respondents to have difficulty answering some of the MBTI questions. For example, some people may state that they are different at work than they are at home—so how should they answer? It is best

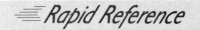

### Rapid Reference

#### 2.1 What to Tell Clients About the MBTI

- The MBTI deals with normal, naturally varying preferences in the ways we acquire information and come to conclusions.
- Questions are best answered according to what is most natural and comfortable, not what a person can do or is required to do.
- The results are designed to be of primary interest and benefit to the client.
- The client is the final judge of the accuracy of the results.
- The MBTI is not a test of skills or abilities, so there are no right or wrong answers and no better or worse results.
- The MBTI does not identify psychological or emotional problems.

to have such a person think about which setting permits or brings out their most natural ways of doing things. For most people, this is likely to be "at home"; for others —"at work" may be the answer.

Past test-taking experience can influence a client's approach to taking the MBTI, and any incorrect assumption about its nature and purposes can be detrimental to the accuracy and usefulness of results. Rapid Reference 2.1 summarizes points to include in initially introducing clients to the MBTI. Some or all of the following tips can help orient clients to taking the instrument:

- Refer to the MBTI as a personality inventory, a questionnaire, or an indicator. Do not refer to it as a test, since the word *test* implies right and wrong answers.
- Explain that the MBTI gives information about natural preferences in how people gather information and how they come to conclusions.
- You can further explain that knowing about one's own and other people's personality preferences can be helpful in areas such as communication and problem solving, career choice, learning styles, personal interests and development, counseling and psychotherapy—depending on why you are asking the client to fill out the Indicator.
- If a client inquires about the forthcoming results, say that results will be in the form of a description of one of 16 possible personality types. The client will assess whether the type he or she reports fits well. If it doesn't, you will help the client identify a better fitting type.

- Advise the client to answer questions according to what is natural and comfortable, not what he or she is capable of doing under pressure.
- Advise clients that they should not think very long about each question; their first, spontaneous response to a question is likely to be the most natural.

### Guidelines During Administration

There is no prescribed time limit for taking the MBTI. Sufficient time should be allotted so that slower respondents will not feel pressured to complete the instrument within the 15 to 25 minutes that is generally needed.

Many respondents do not notice that the question and answer booklet instructions state that omissions are permitted. The rationale for allowing omissions is that if a person truly cannot choose between two options, forcing an answer does not help to identify a preference—it merely adds unreliability to the results. Omitting such an item is preferable to a "guess." However, some respondents may spend so much time considering an item that their automatic, natural response (if they have one) becomes obscured; having been given permission to omit, they may leave out enough items to produce an invalid profile. Three to four omissions on any one dichotomy can produce a problematical scoring situation. The administrator will not know during administration which omissions belong to which dichotomy. If more than three or four omissions are noted overall when the client hands in the filled-out Indicator, it may be ap-

---

## ≡ Rapid Reference

### 2.2 Standard Administration Guidelines

- There is no time limit for taking the MBTI, but it is best not to spend too long on any one item.
- One's immediate response to an item most likely reflects a preference.
- Items can be omitted, but only if it is really not possible to make a choice.
- Do not give the respondent definitions of words or phrases. Suggest the person answer based on his or her own understanding or omit that item.
- Tell a client who is struggling to answer an item that people sometimes feel frustrated when forced to choose; no single item will affect overall results.

propriate to ask the person to consider those questions again, trying for an immediate, "instinctive" response. However, bear in mind that a profile whose validity is in doubt can still serve as a stimulus for helping the client identify his or her type. It is therefore usually best not to "pressure" the respondent to avoid or "correct" omissions.

Rapid Reference 2.2 summarizes these and other basic guidelines during MBTI administration. The first three points should be conveyed just prior to administration; the last two only as they arise during administration.

**Administration Issues Relevant to MBTI Construction**

Respondents sometimes comment on particular features of the MBTI either during or after administration. The most common comments are related to the forced-choice nature of the questions, the simplicity of item wordings, and the fact that item choices are not always logically opposite. The best response to comments in these areas is to agree that being forced to choose is sometimes difficult and frustrating, that the questions do seem too simple to get at anything important, and that options are not always logically opposite. All these "complaints" are due to the goal of identifying people's preferences. Brief explanations such as the ones provided in Rapid Reference 2.3 can be offered in response to these respondent questions.

## ≡ *Rapid Reference*

### 2.3 Common Client Comments and Appropriate Responses

| Client's Comment | Clinician's Response |
|---|---|
| I do both—it's hard to choose one or the other. | Yes, but the questions are asked this way to get at what you generally prefer, not what you are able to do. |
| The questions don't seem to be about anything important. | True. That way most people can answer them, and they do seem to work well to get at people's preferences. |
| Some of the questions are not really opposites. | True. That's because sometimes the exact opposite doesn't get at the right meaning. |

## Special Considerations in a Clinical Setting

It is interesting that an assessment approach developed in a psychotherapeutic context—Carl Jung's clinical practice—is only recently receiving major attention as a valuable tool in the conduct of psychotherapy. Over its lengthy lifespan, the MBTI has been used more often in such areas as career advisement, education, management and organization development, leadership, problem solving, and behavior in teams or groups.

There are some special cautions when administering the MBTI in a clinical setting. The MBTI has low face validity; that is, the questions seem too simplistic to have any bearing on important psychological attributes. The results are in the form of easily understood type descriptions that appear benign and unlikely to harm anyone. Unfortunately, there is a good deal of anecdotal evidence regarding damage done to individuals and group members by a misguided or cavalier use of the MBTI (Pearman, 1993). It is especially important to ensure appropriate administration of the instrument in situations where clients are in distress and vulnerable to concretizing misinformation. Therefore it is recommended that the following information be conveyed to clients before administering the MBTI.

*Results are confidential.* Clients should know that MBTI results will be treated confidentially, just like any other information about them. When administering the MBTI to couples or families, it is usually advisable to give instructions to everyone at the same time and interpret to everyone at the same time, rather than in any individual sessions that may be scheduled. Clinicians should use their own judgment about following this guideline, however, as particular circumstances may make it either practically or therapeutically ill advised. For example, scheduling problems may create unacceptably lengthy delays or added expense for clients; or a clinician may decide that the adolescent children in a particular family should be given feedback separately from their parents.

*Taking the MBTI is voluntary.* The accuracy and usefulness of the MBTI are entirely dependent on obtaining candid responses. A client who is required to fill out the instrument or who feels coerced to do so is unlikely to benefit from the results. Clients should be informed that taking the MBTI is voluntary. Providing the information in Rapid Reference 2.1 generally takes care of any initial resistance to taking the MBTI.

*The MBTI does not identify pathology.* Clients may believe the results will reveal pathological, negative, or unconscious information about them, especially if other instruments they are given appear to deal with pathology. Emphasize the normal, nonpathology basis of type.

## Appropriate Clients

The MBTI may not be an appropriate assessment method for a particular client. Initial considerations involve the likelihood that a valid result will be forthcoming; equally important is whether type information is likely to be useful to the client. The first issue concerns age, reading level, and language; the second is a matter of professional judgment.

### Age and Reading Level Required

An eighth-grade reading level is recommended; questions are generally appropriate for clients who are 14 years of age or older. The Murphy-Meisgeier Type Indicator for Children (Murphy & Meisgeier, 1987) is available for children aged approximately 8 to 14. Chapter 4 suggests uses of the this instrument in conjunction with the MBTI in family therapy. Form M can be used with caution for 12- to 13-year-olds, but they should be told that because the questions were primarily designed for adults, they may not be able to answer some questions and they may omit these questions if necessary. Younger clients are likely to be less clear about their type preferences than more mature people, as was discussed in Chapter 1. Special cautions when verifying and interpreting type with young people are covered in Chapter 4.

### Clients Who Have Difficulty With English

Bilingual practitioners who have non-English-speaking clients or clients whose facility with English poses a problem can consider using one of the available translations of the MBTI. Translations of Form M are not yet commercially available. There are 14 commercial translations of Form G (the previous standard form) and 15 additional Form G translations currently in the research phase. The Spanish (Castellano) commercial translation can be purchased from the publisher, Consulting Psychologists Press; the other translated forms are available from authorized distributors of the MBTI in the relevant countries. For specific information on available translations, see the list of distributors in the publisher's catalog. Clients for whom English is a second language may have some difficulty answering MBTI items that use unfamiliar metaphors. Experience using the American English version (note that there is an European English version developed in the United Kingdom) with clients in non-English-speaking countries indicates that few items cause difficulties and that a valid estimate of type is generally obtained (Myers et al., 1998, chap. 14). However, it is important to use extra care when verifying and interpreting with such clients.

### Visually Impaired Clients

There is no Braille version of the MBTI, but the instrument can be administered to blind people or poor readers by reading the questions aloud, taking care to maintain a neutral tone when reading the options presented.

### Effect of Situational Stress

Moderate to severe stress can influence both a client's willingness to take an instrument like the MBTI as well as the accuracy of the results. People often behave in ways that deviate markedly from their natural type when they are experiencing stress, and this may affect the way they answer MBTI questions. The timing of administration should take the possibility of stress-related distortion into account.

### Clients With Serious Psychological Disturbances

The MBTI was not designed to indicate pathology and is entirely inappropriate for that purpose. However, it can be quite helpful for people suffering from a major psychological disorder to become aware of a natural, healthy part of themselves; such awareness can serve as a vehicle for dealing with important problem areas. Many people who suffer from a variety of psychological disorders are able to provide an accurate report of their natural type. Even when a psychological disturbance does influence the accuracy of self-report, discussing the MBTI with a client can serve a therapeutic purpose.

### Chemically Addicted Clients

The MBTI can be a useful way of encouraging self-understanding and designing effective treatment strategies in a variety of clinical settings, includ-

## CAUTION

### 2.1 Factors That Can Affect the Validity of MBTI Results

The client

- has an inadequate reading or comprehension level.
- is concerned about the purposes to which results will be put.
- is concerned about who will have access to results.
- misunderstands the nature of the instrument.
- wants to please the administrator and answers accordingly.
- is experiencing moderate to severe situational stress.
- has a serious psychological disturbance.
- is actively chemically addicted.

ing treatment for chemical addiction. Caution must be exercised, however, in the timing of administration to these populations. It is generally recommended that the respondent be drug free for at least 30 days prior to administration. A shorter interval risks substantial distortion of self-perception as a result of the addiction itself. Caution 2.1 summarizes this and other client factors that can affect the validity of MBTI results.

## Appropriate Administrators

In many clinical settings the practitioner explains, solicits cooperation, selects a scoring option, and interprets the MBTI to an individual client, couple, or family. In other settings the MBTI may be part of a battery of self-administered instruments given to the client at intake. This latter situation poses important administration issues that may impact the validity of results and require special cautions when giving feedback to clients. To minimize such effects, try one or both of the following suggestions:

1. Emphasize to the person responsible for administering instruments that the client must *read all instructions on the MBTI test form.*
2. Consider removing the MBTI from the battery and administering it later. Because many clients are in a highly stressed state at intake, this reduces the likelihood of obtaining an accurate self-report. In general, administering the MBTI at the very beginning of therapy is not recommended. It is usually best to wait for evidence that an initial crisis state has abated. An exception may be with couples or

in family therapy: The MBTI can often provide a positive and neutral ground from which to address serious relationship problems. Make sure to caution all concerned that they must not discuss the questions or their responses with each other as they fill out the Indicator.

### Ethical Guidelines for MBTI Administration

Standard ethical issues and guidelines apply to the MBTI just as they do to administration of other psychological instruments. In addition, the guiding principle of providing results directly to the client promotes some additional recommendations. Don't Forget 2.1 reproduces a portion of *Ethical Principles* developed by the Association for Psychological Type, a membership organization consisting of professionals from a variety of disciplines who use the MBTI in their work with clients. Chapter 4 includes sections of this document that are relevant to verification and interpretation of the MBTI.

---

## DON'T FORGET

### 2.1 Ethical Guidelines Regarding Administration and Dissemination of MBTI Results

#### Principle I. Administration and Dissemination of Results

Information about a person's type should be acquired and used so as to be of maximum benefit to the individual.

1. The respondent to a type indicator should, in all instances, be informed of the purpose and intended use of results prior to taking the instrument. Taking the instrument should be voluntary.

2. Identified type results (as distinguished from grouped data) may not be given to a person other than the individual taking the instrument, without that individual's prior permission.

    2a. In an organizational context, type information should be used to enhance individual and group satisfaction, rather than to restrict or limit individual or group functioning.

*continued*

3. In providing type results to respondents, adequate information about psychological type theory and the individual's own indicated type should be provided in a face-to-face setting. Results should not be given in impersonal ways, such as through the mail.

3a. Information regarding psychological type theory and type results may be given individually or in a group setting. However, individuals should be given an opportunity to clarify their indicated type with the practitioner. Practitioners are encouraged to provide, at a minimum, a full written description of the indicated type, such as is contained in *Introduction to Type* (Myers, 1998).

3b. In situations where type data are being used for research purposes only, giving individual results to respondents is not required. However, researchers are encouraged to provide the option for feedback based on individual request.

*Note.* From "Ethical Principles," Association for Psychological Type (1992, pp. 1–3). Used with permission.

## Choosing the Right Form of the Instrument

All versions of Form M contain 93 items and take 15 to 25 minutes to complete. Unlike Form G and its predecessors, there are no nonscored research items on Form M. Deciding on which version of the MBTI to administer depends on the purposes for which it is being given as well as on time, situation, and financial constraints. Versions of the Indicator include a self-scorable form, one that is template (hand) scorable, and several computer-scoring options. Chapter 3 provides the information necessary for deciding on the kind of administration that is appropriate in different situations, and Chapter 4 discusses interpretation issues that may impact choice of MBTI form.

There is a critical guideline that applies to the order in which administration, scoring, and interpretation take place for individual clients as well as in groups. The recommended order and associated guidelines relevant to the administration phase of the procedure are covered in greater detail in Chapters 3 and 4.

## Computerized Versions of Form M

The computer-scored form of the MBTI can be administered in the following ways:

1. The client marks answers on the printed booklet/answer sheet, which is sent to Consulting Psychologists Press for scoring.
2. The client answers the items presented on a computer screen.
3. The client marks answers on the printed booklet/answer sheet, and the responses are then keyed in.
4. The client answers on the Internet on a system licensed to the practitioner.

The most current information about computer-based administration of the MBTI is available in both the publisher's catalog and web page. The web site is www.mbti.com.

## 🦅 TEST YOURSELF 🦅

**I. What is the time limit for taking the MBTI?**

(a) 25 minutes

(b) 40 minutes

(c) There is no time limit.

(d) It depends on the form of the instrument being used.

**2. Clients diagnosed as borderline should never be given the MBTI.** True or False?

**3. Which of the following is *not* an acceptable administration technique?**

(a) reading the questions aloud to someone who reads poorly

(b) encouraging respondents to "go with" their first reaction

(c) defining a word for a 14-year-old respondent

(d) saying that it is okay to omit an item

**4. It is advisable that clients who are being treated for chemical addiction**

(a) be drug free for a minimum of 30 days before taking the MBTI.

(b) take the MBTI at intake into the treatment program.

(c) be drug free for at least 3 months before taking the MBTI.

(d) take the MBTI only at completion of treatment.

**5. Seriously disturbed clients rarely provide a valid MBTI profile.** True or False?

*continued*

6. **The reading level recommended for using the MBTI is**
   (a) 6th grade.
   (b) 8th grade.
   (c) 10th grade.
   (d) 12th grade.

7. **With regard to administering the MBTI to people for whom English is a second language,**
   (a) it is definitely best to use the appropriate translation if there is one available.
   (b) the person will be unlikely to report type accurately regardless of which form is used.
   (c) the English version is likely to yield valid results.
   (d) cultural differences make use of the Indicator with these people questionable.

8. **It is appropriate for respondents who are family members to discuss their answers with each other while they are filling out the Indicator.** True or False?

9. **All 93 items on MBTI Form M are used for identifying four-letter type.** True or False?

10. **Confidentiality requirements include providing interpretation feedback individually to each partner in a couple.** True or False?

11. **Situational stress at the time of MBTI administration may influence results.** True or False?

12. **What is a frequent issue for clients when answering the MBTI?**
    (a) It is hard to choose between only two things.
    (b) They do both things at different times.
    (c) The questions are so simple they can't get at anything important.
    (d) all of the above

13. **The estimated time for completing Form M is**
    (a) 15 to 25 minutes for the computer-scored version; 30-40 minutes for self-scorable and template-scorable versions.
    (b) 25 to 35 minutes for the computer-scored; 40-50 minutes for self-scorable and template-scorable versions.
    (c) 15 to 25 minutes for all versions of the Form M.
    (d) 25 to 35 minutes for all versions.

**14. What points are advisable to make to a client prior to administration?**

**15. What frame of mind should you recommend to clients as they answer the Indicator questions?**

*Answers:* 1. c; 2. False; 3. c; 4. a; 5. False; 6. a; 7. c; 8. False; 9. a; 10. False; 11. True; 12. d; 13. c; 14. Normal personality characteristics; preferences, not skills; results designed for client; does not identify psychological problems; 15. What you prefer when you are most free to act according to your inclinations.

Three

# HOW TO SCORE THE MBTI

The primary goal in scoring the Myers-Briggs Type Indicator personality inventory is to assign the client to four categories: E or I, S or N, T or F, and J or P. With the introduction of Form M in 1998, use of the term *score* is discouraged, both in explaining type to clients and in "thinking about" type results. The kinds of scores that were reported on previous forms of the Indicator inadvertently encouraged their misinterpretation as traitlike measures of use, competence, maturity, or accessibility. Form M has one measure that is referenced as a score and another that is termed points.

Theta ($\theta$) scores are generated by item response theory computer scoring of the MBTI. Theta scores are the basis of the preference clarity index, which is reported to the client at the professional's discretion. Theta scores are the equivalent of the continuous scores that were calculated on previous MBTI forms and used for research purposes. Computer scoring provides researchers with the theta scores needed for various research methodologies. Theta scores permit assignment of respondents to type categories according to cutoff points determined for each dichotomy. The resulting four-letter type is the principle result reported to clients. Theta scores themselves are not reported to the client.

Raw points apply only to the self-scorable and template-scored versions of the MBTI. Raw points are not interpreted in themselves; they are used to generate the preference clarity index and preference clarity category, both of which are estimates of the clarity with which a respondent reports the categorical preference in question. On previous forms of the Indicator, points were the basis for calculating the preference scores and continuous scores that were reported.

## ESTIMATES OF CLARITY OF PREFERENCE

In devising MBTI Form M, much care was taken to discourage both practitioners and clients from assuming that the numbers associated with MBTI preferences are interpretable as amounts of, degrees of competence with, levels of maturity of use, or relative ease of access to these preferences. To mitigate such misinterpretations, the interdependent concepts of preference clarity index and preference clarity category were developed. Both terms provide estimates of the clarity with which a client has reported a preference on a particular administration of the MBTI.

### The Preference Clarity Index

For all dichotomies, the preference clarity index ranges from 1 to 30. An index closer to 30 indicates that the respondent has consistently answered the MBTI items on that dichotomy in favor of the preferred pole; an index closer to 1 means that the respondent has answered nearly as many items favoring the nonpreferred pole as the preferred pole. Alternative interpretive possibilities that can be explored with a client are discussed in Chapter 4. Inferences about the possible meaning of an individual's clarity of preference are not warranted in the absence of additional information. Rapid Reference 3.1 shows the ranges that are associated with the four categories of preference clarity.

The preference clarity index is computed and reported only on computer-scored versions of MBTI Form M. Reporting the actual number to the client

## ≡ *Rapid Reference*

### 3.1 Clarity of Preference as Estimated by the Preference Clarity Index

| Preference Clarity Index | Preference Clarity Category |
|---|---|
| 26–30 | Very clear |
| 16–25 | Clear |
| 6–15 | Moderate |
| 1–5 | Slight |

without carefully explaining its meaning is not helpful. Practitioners are better advised to give clients preference clarity category information as described below. Chapter 4 presents the rationale for caution in interpreting MBTI results.

## The Preference Clarity Category

Preference clarity categories are reported to the client as "very clear," "clear," "moderate," and "slight," as indicated in Rapid Reference 3.1. For self-scored and template-scored versions of the MBTI, the preference clarity category is determined by the range of raw points that are associated with each preference, rather than being associated with the preference clarity index of the computer-scored version. Rapid Reference 3.2 shows how to convert raw points to preference clarity categories. Note that there are

## ≡Rapid Reference

### 3.2 Converting Raw Points into Preference Clarity Categories

| Dichotomy | Greatest Raw Points | Preference Clarity Category |
|---|---|---|
| E–I | 11–13 | Slight |
|  | 14–16 | Moderate |
|  | 17–19 | Clear |
|  | 20–21 | Very clear |
| S–N | 13–15 | Slight |
|  | 16–20 | Moderate |
|  | 21–24 | Clear |
|  | 25–26 | Very clear |
| T–F | 12–14 | Slight |
|  | 15–18 | Moderate |
|  | 19–22 | Clear |
|  | 23–24 | Very clear |

continued

| Dichotomy | Greatest Raw Points | Preference Clarity Category |
|---|---|---|
| J–P | 11–13 | Slight |
| | 14–16 | Moderate |
| | 17–20 | Clear |
| | 21–22 | Very clear |

*Note.* Equal points on E–I is classified as *I*; equal points on S–N is classified as *N*; equal points on T–F is classified as *F*; equal points on J–P is classified as *P*. Also note that if items have been omitted on a scale, the highest raw points may be lower than the range shown. Use "slight" for the pcc if this occurs. From Myers et al. (1998, p. 112). Modified and reproduced by special permission of the Publisher, Consulting Psychologists Press, Inc., Palo Alto, CA 94303 from *MBTI® Manual: A Guide to the Development and Use of the Myers-Briggs Type Indicator*, Third Edition by Isabel Briggs Myers, Mary H. McCaulley, Naomi L. Quenk, and Allen L. Hammer. Copyright 1998 by Consulting Psychologists Press, Inc. All rights reserved. Further reproduction is prohibited without the Publisher's written consent.

slightly different raw point ranges for each of the dichotomies, unlike preference category index–generated clarity ranges, which are the same for each dichotomy.

## CAUTION

### 3.1 Appropriate Steps for Administering and Scoring the MBTI

1. Tell the client what the MBTI is about, as in Rapid Reference 2.1.
2. Have the client answer the MBTI.
3. Score the MBTI, but *do not* give the results to the client. In the case of the self-scorable form, *do not allow* members of the client group to score the form yet.

## SCORING OPTIONS

The available MBTI scoring options require administration of the particular form that will produce the scoring option you want. The computer-scored form can also be scored by hand using a special set of templates. Such template scoring yields an approximation of the precise IRT scoring. The self-scorable form is not suitable for computer scoring. However, the standard nonprepaid template-scorable form can be upgraded to the more precise IRT computer

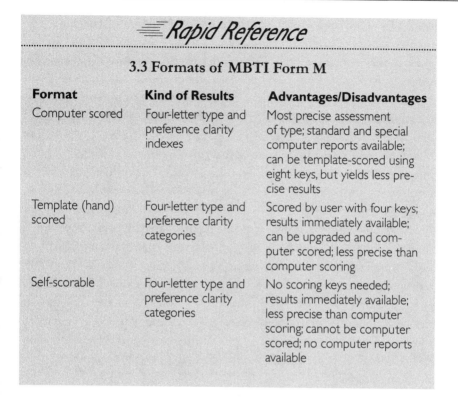

## ≡ Rapid Reference

### 3.3 Formats of MBTI Form M

| Format | Kind of Results | Advantages/Disadvantages |
|---|---|---|
| Computer scored | Four-letter type and preference clarity indexes | Most precise assessment of type; standard and special computer reports available; can be template-scored using eight keys, but yields less precise results |
| Template (hand) scored | Four-letter type and preference clarity categories | Scored by user with four keys; results immediately available; can be upgraded and computer scored; less precise than computer scoring |
| Self-scorable | Four-letter type and preference clarity categories | No scoring keys needed; results immediately available; less precise than computer scoring; cannot be computer scored; no computer reports available |

scoring; the various computer reports can then be provided. Your scoring choice for a particular client or client group will depend on issues of convenience, cost, flexibility in administration, and purposes to which the results will be put. Some practitioners use one option exclusively; others may keep several forms on hand to meet different client needs. Regardless of which scoring option you use, the order of steps recommended from administration through scoring will be the one shown in Caution 3.1.

Rapid Reference 3.3 shows the several different ways that Standard Form M can be administered, the results each yields, and their advantages and/or disadvantages.

## Computer Scoring

One booklet contains both questions and space for answers on the computer-scored form. Computer scoring uses an item response theory method. Earlier forms of the Indicator used a prediction ratio method for selecting and scoring items. Item response theory methods are based on modern test theory, whereas the prediction ratio method fits within classical test theory approaches. Research comparing the two methods showed that item response theory yields higher internal consistency reliabilities and is also more likely to identify the type that "best fits" the respondent. The item response theory method *requires* computer scoring, because it evaluates the contribution of each item to the resulting type, a task that can only be accomplished by computer. Classical test theory evaluates scales rather than individual items and is not dependent on the computer for scoring. Both the template- and self-scorable versions of MBTI Form M yield an *approximation* of item response theory scoring, rather than item response theory–based precision of sorting at the midpoint. It is therefore possible for computer scoring and template scoring of the same answer sheet to report two different types, even though the percentage agreement between the two scoring options ranges from 93.8 for Extraversion to 99.3 for Sensing (Myers et al. 1998). All methods of scoring previous standard forms of the Indicator yielded identical results in identifying four-letter type and in associated scores. The prediction ratio method of scoring used on previous forms permitted computer scoring but did not require it for greater precision.

## Scoring the Computer Form With Templates

The computer form can be hand scored using a set of eight templates—one for each preference pole. Template scoring is useful in situations where you want a quick estimate of your client's type—sooner than computer results will be available. Detailed, easy-to-follow scoring instructions appear on each of the templates. Template scoring requires placing each of the eight templates on each of the three booklet pages, recording the raw points for each preference pole on each page, and adding the results together to obtain the total raw points for each preference pole. With a little experience, this takes about 10 minutes. The pole of each dichotomy that has the larger number of raw points identifies the respondent's preference on that dichotomy.

Equal points are classified as I, N, F, or P, depending on the dichotomy. The convention of breaking tied scores in this fashion was set by Isabel Briggs Myers when she constructed previous forms of the Indicator. The basic rationale is that ties are broken in favor of the preference pole that is *less* common or sanctioned in the population at large: A person with "split votes" on a dichotomy is indicating a "pull" toward the less popular pole, which may be counteracted by an equal "pull" toward the more popular pole. The likely preference is therefore hypothesized to be the less popular one. In this reasoning, for example, a person with equal points for E and I is "going against the tide" that favors an extraverted approach and is therefore probably truly an Introvert struggling to accommodate to what is socially desirable.

It is important to be aware that tie breaking is a technical device that enables each MBTI record to be classified as one of the 16 types. From a practical interpretation standpoint (as detailed in Chapter 4), an equal-point situation on any dichotomy signals that extra care in verifying the preference is required.

The raw point value for a preference enables determination of the preference clarity category, which as described earlier ranges from "slight" to "very clear." A conversion table appropriate to the particular dichotomy appears on each template. It enables you to determine the preference clarity category for preferences on that dichotomy. Note that a summary of the conversions for all dichotomies was shown in Rapid Reference 3.2. The information in that Rapid Reference also applies to conversion of points for standard template scoring and the self-scorable version of the Indicator, which are described below.

## Standard Template Scoring

Practitioners who do not require the precision of computer scoring and do not need the convenience of the self-scorable form may prefer this scoring option. Reusable question booklets and separate individual answer sheets are used. Scoring is accomplished using four templates, one for each dichotomy. Each template has instructions for scoring both poles of the dichotomy in question, which involves matching openings in the template to asterisks that appear on the answer sheet and counting the raw points for each pole. As was described for template scoring of the computer form, the pole of each dichotomy that has the larger number of raw points identifies the respondent's preference on that dichotomy. The raw point value for that preference is used to determine the preference clarity category, ranging from "slight" to "very clear," as was indicated in Rapid Reference 3.2. Template scoring of Form M is simpler, faster, and has less possibility of error than was the case for template scoring of Form G: There are four templates used rather than five, which are needed for Form G; all items receive only 1 point, whereas for Form G, items were weighted 0, 1, or 2.

## Self-Scorable Form

A combined question-and-answer booklet that is not reusable is used for the self-scorable version of the MBTI. The self-scorable form is designed to be administered and scored in a group setting. It is generally not used for administration to individual clients. However, practitioners who are concerned about the confidentiality issues that could arise if MBTI results are included in an employee's file might consider using the self-scorable form with individuals and having clients retain their results so that there will be no permanent record in employee files.

To answer the self-scorable form, the respondent marks an $X$ in the selected box for each question. When all items are answered (and after the group has had an opportunity to self-assess type), the respondent opens the perforation and turns the page. Instructions on the form direct the respondent to count and record the number of marks in each row. Totals for columns give the raw points for each preference pole. Looking at each dichotomy separately, the preference pole with the larger raw point value is recorded as the preference on that dichotomy. In that way the respondent finds his or her four-letter type. If desired, an estimate of clarity of preference (preference clarity category) can be obtained using the information in Rapid Reference 3.2. When using the self-scorable form, it is important to collect the actual question-and-answer booklets before clients leave the room to prevent respondents from "administering" the questions and "scoring" people who did not attend the MBTI session. Respondents should be encouraged to make a note of their four-letter type and their self-assessment, probably together with the interpretation materials given to them during the feedback session. The exception to this recommendation was described earlier for employees in situations where the risk of clients "administering" the form to others may be outweighed by potential misuse of the information within an organization. Of course, both goals can be accomplished by having each person record individual results, collecting the self-scorable forms, and immediately destroying them.

## Computer-Generated Profiles and Reports

Written feedback to supplement face-to-face interpretation of MBTI results is available in several profiles and reports that can be obtained by administering the correct computer-scored answer sheets. Answer sheets can then be sent to the publisher for scoring and reports, or on site if you are using the Consulting Psychologists Press software system or the Consulting Psychologists Press web administration site, which are described below. The specific profiles and reports are described in Chapter 4.

### Software

A Microsoft Windows environment is needed to use the Consulting Psychologists Press software system, which is available under license from the publisher. After responses are entered, the reports desired can be printed immediately, providing the practitioner has selected those report options for the software system being used. The printed reports can then be used as part of the verification and interpretation procedure.

### Using the Internet

The MBTI can be administered on the Internet and also scored as part of that service, using the Consulting Psychologists Press web administration site under license from the publisher. A major asset of this option is that professionals can provide MBTI assessment to clients in remote locations. The same reports available on the software option can be printed using web site administration. Note, however, that interpretation guidelines require that standard interpretation procedures be followed in giving results to clients who take the Indicator on the World Wide Web, just as they do for other settings and modes of administration. Specific information on Internet delivery of the MBTI can be found in the publisher's catalog.

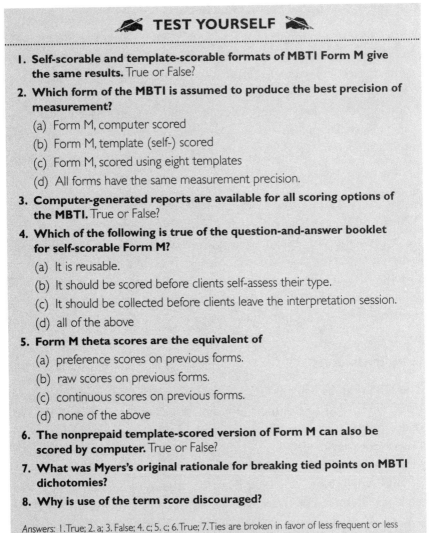

### 🖋 TEST YOURSELF 🖋

1. **Self-scorable and template-scorable formats of MBTI Form M give the same results.** True or False?

2. **Which form of the MBTI is assumed to produce the best precision of measurement?**
   (a) Form M, computer scored
   (b) Form M, template (self-) scored
   (c) Form M, scored using eight templates
   (d) All forms have the same measurement precision.

3. **Computer-generated reports are available for all scoring options of the MBTI.** True or False?

4. **Which of the following is true of the question-and-answer booklet for self-scorable Form M?**
   (a) It is reusable.
   (b) It should be scored before clients self-assess their type.
   (c) It should be collected before clients leave the interpretation session.
   (d) all of the above

5. **Form M theta scores are the equivalent of**
   (a) preference scores on previous forms.
   (b) raw scores on previous forms.
   (c) continuous scores on previous forms.
   (d) none of the above

6. **The nonprepaid template-scored version of Form M can also be scored by computer.** True or False?

7. **What was Myers's original rationale for breaking tied points on MBTI dichotomies?**

8. **Why is use of the term *score* discouraged?**

*Answers:* 1. True; 2. a; 3. False; 4. c; 5. c; 6. True; 7. Ties are broken in favor of less frequent or less socially sanctioned preference; 8. To discourage a "skill" or "frequency of use" interpretation.

Four

# HOW TO INTERPRET THE MBTI

Interpretation of the Myers-Briggs Type Indicator personality inventory differs from the interpretation of other assessment instruments because the initial step is to have the client verify the accuracy of the results obtained. Once this has been accomplished, the interpretation can focus on the impact of a client's type in an area of interest. Effective interpretation of the MBTI requires a knowledge of type theory, the psychometric properties of the MBTI, and what can and cannot be legitimately inferred from an individual's MBTI results. The first part of this chapter focuses on type verification, including the rationale for verifying type, the step-by-step procedure for accomplishing the task, resources for verifying and interpreting type to clients, and caveats when verifying type with particular kinds of clients. The second part is a discussion of various issues that have an impact on the interpretation of a client's type, such as gender expectations.

## TYPE VERIFICATION

Minimizing the sources of error is a major goal in constructing any assessment tool. When tests are individually administered, the clinician can obtain valuable clues about factors that may influence the validity of obtained results, and take those into account when interpreting test results for that individual. This source of information is generally absent when using self-administered tests like the MBTI, although respondents' spontaneous comments about the experience of answering a test can be useful. Regardless of whether a test is administered by a professional or self-administered, rarely is the respondent asked to evaluate the validity of test results, and it is even more unusual to interpret test results based on the client's assessment rather than actual test results. As a self-report instrument with a forced-choice format and low face validity, the MBTI is subject to a number of factors that can influence its accuracy. A clinician who keeps these in mind can find them useful in understanding an individual client's personality development and mode of functioning. That self-report results are subject to error is also the underlying motivation for verifying type results. Don't Forget 4.1 summarizes factors that can contribute to a client reporting a type that differs from the type that is later verified.

## Rationale for Verifying Type Results

We can usually assume that if a test has been properly administered and accurately scored, the results are probably valid. The studies referred to later in this section certainly suggest that the MBTI is likely to yield accurate type results, although this depends in part on the criteria used to define accuracy. Most studies of this issue compare MBTI results to one or another method of having respondents appraise their own type either prior to seeing their MBTI results, after reviewing those results, or a combination of both pre- and post-self-assessment. A common methodology involves some variation on the following four steps, which also represents the general type verification method recommended later in this section.

1. The MBTI is administered and scored. This yields a respondent's "reported type."
2. The type approach to personality and the four dichotomies are explained and described to respondents, either verbally, using written materials, or with a combination of verbal and written material.

3. Respondents self-assess to arrive at each of their four preferences based on the explanation.

4. Respondents are asked to read the type description that corresponds to their MBTI results and possibly one or more additional type descriptions that may be likely alternatives. They are then asked to identify which type best describes them. This yields the "best fit type."

Studies that have used some variation of this four-point process of comparing reported type to best fit type are not strictly comparable because of wide variations in the nature of samples and sample sizes. Largely uncontrolled variables such as the variety of verification methods and materials used for self-assessment also make comparisons difficult. Acknowledging these drawbacks, agreement across such studies on three of the four MBTI preferences ranges from 90% to 99%, and agreement on all four preferences ranges from 53% to 85% (Myers et al., 1998, pp. 117, 197). These levels of accuracy are quite supportive of the validity of the MBTI in eliciting type when self-assessment is the criterion used. This is especially notable when we consider that the chance likelihood of reporting or of self-assessing as any one of the 16 types is 6.25%. The MBTI stands up well to this criterion of validity. However, because the overriding goal is to enable individuals to understand their own four-letter type as a dynamic construct, results that are "much better than chance" or even "correct on three out of four categories" are not adequate. Additional efforts are needed to help individuals verify the type they reported or identify an alternative best fit type.

The definitions of reported type, best fit type, and a third notion, true type, are as follows:

- *Reported type.* This is the type that results from an administration of the MBTI. It tells us the way the respondent answered the questions on one particular occasion. Bear in mind that the instrument is labeled an indicator rather than a test not only to discourage the idea that it has right and wrong answers, but also because it is meant to indicate which type is *likely* to best fit the respondent.
- *Best fit type.* This is the type that the client decides describes him or her best, after a standard type verification session such as is detailed in this

chapter. The ultimate goal of type verification is to arrive at the client's best fit type.

- *True type.* This is a hypothetical construct, similar to the notion of true score on a test. It is assumed that a person's true type is never known with absolute certainty.

## Minimizing Interpreter Type Bias

Knowing one's own results on the Wechsler Adult Intelligence Scale (WAIS) is not required to effectively interpret the WAIS; taking the Minnesota Multiphasic Personality Inventory, Rorschach, or Draw-a-Person tests are not mandated in order for a clinician to interpret these tests. With the MBTI, however, a basic assumption is that the interpreter of the instrument has taken the MBTI, had it appropriately interpreted, and has verified a type, either the type reported at administration or a different one determined as a result of the verification process. Professionals will therefore make the most effective use of this book when they have verified their own type and have a complete set of type descriptions available for reference.

The rationale for self-awareness of type is that knowing one's own type helps the interpreter avoid biases in explaining type to the client and in interpreting the client's type in relation to the area of concern. This is important because the way both laypeople and professionals understand and evaluate others is strongly influenced by their own type perspective and/or a societal notion of psychological health and adaptation. For example, an unaware interpreter with a preference for Intuition can convey to a client that Intuition is superior to Sensing; an Introverted interpreter can present Extraverts as overbearing and shallow. In clinical settings in particular, assessments may be colored by the clinician's personal type perspective. For example, an unaware ENFP psychologist may evaluate an ISTJ client as "overly" meticulous and "obsessed with" details, reflecting her dislike and devaluing of the less preferred aspects of her own type—and her misunderstanding of the natural strengths and competencies of well-functioning ISTJs. In a similar way, societal biases can emerge when a clinician assumes that types that are characterized as ambitious, self-directed, and goal oriented are "better adapted" or "emotionally healthier" than types who prefer to stay in the background and dislike leadership roles.

## Guidelines for Type Verification

Once the MBTI has been administered according to the procedures described in Chapter 2 and in the order recommended in Caution 2.2, and you have scored the instrument as described in Chapter 3 and Caution 3.1, the next step, as shown in Caution 4.1, is type verification and interpretation.

A first requirement for helping others verify their types is to acknowledge that one's own perspective is only one of 16 equally valid ones and thus to recognize one's potential for bias. An associated prerequisite is to develop facility in describing the poles of each type dichotomy and the 16 whole types in the most neutral and positive manner possible. Achieving perfect neutrality is not a realistic goal for any interpreter, but maintaining vigilance about one's own and others' type biases is both possible as well as professionally and personally illuminating.

---

## CAUTION

### 4.1 Appropriate Steps From Administration Through Interpretation

1. Tell the client what the MBTI is about, as in Rapid Reference 2.1.
2. Have the client answer the MBTI.
3. Score the MBTI using one of the methods described in Chapter 3, but *do not* give the results to the client. In the case of the self-scorable form, *do not allow members of the client group to score the form yet.*
4. Give the client an opportunity to self-assess and verify his or her type, using standard procedures described in this chapter.
5. Interpret verified MBTI results in relation to the area of interest.

---

## Step-by-Step Type Verification

### Step 1. Explain What a "Preference" Is

The very first step in type verification is to explain the idea of a natural personality preference and distinguish it from a learned and practiced skill. Many clients confuse what they *can* do with what they *prefer* to do. A helpful exercise to clarify the differences uses the analogy of right- and left-handedness. The exercise is as follows.

1. Have the client sign his or her name on an ordinary piece of paper. (This will typically be done with the preferred hand.)

2. Ask the client to sign again, this time using the other hand.

3. Ask the client, "What was it like to sign the first time with your preferred hand?" "What was it like signing the second time with your nonpreferred hand?"

4. Typically, comments about the preferred hand include natural, automatic, quick, easy, legible. Comments about the nonpreferred hand include awkward, had to think about it, slow, difficult, childlike.

5. Point out that our experience using our preferred and nonpreferred hands is an excellent way of describing preferred and nonpreferred parts of our personality. One of each pair of opposites is experienced as natural, comfortable, and satisfying; when we are required to use the opposite, less preferred part of ourselves, though we *can* do it, it is with some degree of awkwardness, discomfort, and reduced confidence and often results in less satisfaction with the outcome.

6. Point out that if for some reason the client had to use his or her nonpreferred hand exclusively for a period of time, he or she could probably do so, but the extra effort required might be tiring and dissatisfying. The same is true when we are required to use a less preferred part of our personality for an extended period of time.

The analogies in the exercise are very helpful at a variety of points in the verification and interpretation process. Returning to these points and reinforcing them can help discourage misinterpreting the preferences as learned skills. The notion of what comes naturally versus what takes effort and is fatiguing can help resolve a less clear reported preference on any dichotomy.

### Step 2. Explain the Opposite Poles of Each Dichotomy

It is a good idea to orient your explanations to suit the age, education, and probable interests of your client or client group. Beginning with brief definitions of the opposites such as are included in Rapid Reference 1.3 is a good place to start. Many practitioners present the dichotomies in the order shown there, which is also the order in which the letters appear in any type code. Others prefer to present the two pairs of functions (Sensing and Intuition; Thinking and Feeling) followed by the two pairs of attitudes (Extraversion and Introversion; Judging and Perceiving). This latter order lends itself most readily to an explanation of the dynamic character of type; it leads naturally to the notion that the functions and attitudes do not operate independently of one another—one doesn't simply extravert or introvert; one extraverts or introverts Sensing or Intuition, or Thinking, or Feeling at any particular time.

Regardless of the order of presentation used, initial verification should fo-

## ≡ *Rapid Reference*

### 4.1 How to Explain Extraversion and Introversion

- Extraversion and Introversion are two opposite ways of being energized and using energy. When we are extraverting, we direct our energy mainly outwardly, toward people and objects in the outside world; it is natural when we are extraverting to *take action* in relation to people and events. When we are introverting, we direct our energy mainly inwardly, toward our inner experiences and ideas; it is natural when we are introverting to *reflect* before we take action.

- Everyone uses both Extraversion and Introversion at least some of the time, but one of the pair tends to be most natural and automatic—as we saw with our handedness exercise.

- People who prefer Extraversion typically feel energized by and seek out situations where they can work with or socialize with people and be actively involved with the world. When they spend a great deal of time alone they may feel tired, dissatisfied, out of sorts, and they may seek out the stimulation of other people and activities; they *extravert* to reenergize.

- People who prefer Introversion typically feel energized by and seek out situations where can they work alone or spend recreational time alone, and where they have plenty of time to reflect on what they are doing. If they have to spend a great deal of time working with, being around, or socializing with people, they may feel tired, dissatisfied, out of sorts, and they may seek out the quiet and restfulness of being alone; they *introvert* to reenergize.

Ask the client to consider the following questions:

1. Do you have a sense of which you prefer and how you answered the MBTI?

2. What are some ways that you typically use _____? (Extraversion or Introversion—whichever the person prefers)

3. When and in what ways do you use _____? (the non-preferred pole)

If the preference is unclear after further discussion, ask:

4. Are you more likely to yearn for solitude after being active and around people, or do you seek outside stimulation when you have been alone for a long time?

## *Rapid Reference*

### 4.2 How to Explain Sensing and Intuition

- Sensing and Intuition are two opposite ways of gathering information or perceiving. When we use Sensing, we gather information through our five senses; when we are using Sensing it is natural to notice the facts and details that are in our immediate environment. When we use Intuition, we focus on patterns and meanings that can be inferred from information obtained through our senses; it is natural when we use Intuition to speculate about future possibilities and implications.

- Everyone uses both Sensing and Intuition at least some of the time, but one of the pair tends to be most natural and automatic.

- People who prefer Sensing typically notice and remember facts and details; they like information to be firmly connected to past and present experience and prefer situations that are grounded, clear-cut, with facts that can be readily verified. They can become impatient and critical when forced to deal with ambiguity and conjecture. Finding ways to engage their Sensing preference helps restore their equilibrium.

- People who prefer Intuition typically read "between the lines," making inferences about the meaning of others' words and actions. They prefer situations that allow them to speculate about future possibilities and can become bored and unmotivated when forced to deal with facts and details. Finding ways to engage their Intuition helps restore equilibrium.

Ask the client to consider the following questions:

1. Do you have a sense of which you prefer and how you answered the MBTI?

2. What are some ways that you typically use _____? (Sensing or Intuition—whichever the person prefers)

3. When and in what ways do you use _____? (the non-preferred pole)

If the preference is unclear after further discussion, ask:

4. Overall, when you are most able to do as you like, are you more likely to notice and remember the details of a new situation and figure out what it means later, or do you first get an overall impression of what is going on and think about specifics later?

cus on helping clients identify which of each pair of opposites they prefer. The clinician might say, "I'm going to explain both of the opposite ways of 'gathering information'" (or "coming to conclusions" or "being energized" or "relating to the outside world," depending on which dichotomy is being explained. Rapid References 4.1, 4.2, 4.3, and 4.4 summarize and build on the

## ≡ Rapid Reference

### 4.3 How to Explain Thinking and Feeling

- Thinking and Feeling are two opposite ways of making judgments and coming to conclusions. Remember that on the MBTI, Thinking doesn't mean "smart" and Feeling doesn't mean "emotional"; in fact, intelligence and emotionality are outside of the type system. When we use Thinking, we use objective criteria and cause-and-effect analysis to reach a conclusion that is logically true. When we use Feeling, we weigh our own and others' values and concerns to reach a conclusion that promotes agreement and harmony among those involved.

- Everyone uses both Thinking and Feeling at least some of the time, but the one that is used most automatically and naturally is the one preferred.

- People who prefer Thinking typically take a dispassionate approach to decision making, using consistent principles and objective criteria to arrive at conclusions that treat people impartially; this is their primary goal and the welfare of people is secondary.

- People who prefer Feeling typically involve themselves in the decision-making situation, working to understand the values and concerns of those involved in order to arrive at conclusions that take the welfare of people into account as the primary goal, with logic and impartiality being secondary.

Ask the client to consider the following questions:

1. Do you have a sense of which you prefer and how you answered the MBTI? [As an interpreter, be aware that of the four dichotomies, this one is most influenced by gender expectations. In addition, many work settings favor a Thinking approach.]

2. What are some ways that you typically use _____? (Thinking or Feeling—whichever the person prefers)

3. When and in what ways do you use _____? (the non-preferred pole)

If the preference is unclear after further discussion, ask:

4. Overall, when you are most able to do as you like, does what is logical and objective occur to you first, or does concern about the impacts on people occur to you first?

definitions in Chapter 1 and include queries to help clients identify their preference and help them recognize that they can and do use nonpreferred poles of each dichotomy, but probably less comfortably and enthusiastically than when using the preferred pole. Note that each pole of a dichotomy is described by the qualities that make it legitimate in its own right; one pole is *not*

## ≡ Rapid Reference

### 4.4 How to Explain Judging and Perceiving Attitudes

- Judging and Perceiving are two opposite attitudes—general approaches taken when we deal with the outer, extraverted world—regardless of whether we prefer Extraversion or Introversion. Remember that the term *Judging* does not mean judgmental and the term *Perceiving* does not mean perceptive. When we use a Judging attitude, we want things in the outer world to be settled and decided; it is natural when we take a Judging attitude to use our Thinking or Feeling judgment (whichever we prefer) to be organized, methodical, and to reach decisions quickly. When we use a Perceiving attitude, we want to gather as much information as possible before we reach a decision; it is natural when we take a Perceiving attitude to use our Sensing or Intuition (whichever we prefer) to be flexible, spontaneous, and to reach decisions only after considering many options.

- Everyone uses both a Judging and a Perceiving attitude at least some of the time, but the one that we use most comfortably when we can behave as we like is likely to be our natural preference.

- People who prefer a Judging attitude typically like to make both short- and long-term plans and get things done efficiently, according to a schedule. They would rather make a decision that has to be changed later than indefinitely put off decision making to gather more information.

- People who prefer a Perceiving attitude typically like the freedom to respond spontaneously and flexibly to tasks and feel most effective without set plans. They would rather consider all the relevant information available before making a decision than to come to closure with insufficient information.

Ask the client to consider the following questions:

1. Do you have a sense of which you prefer and how you answered the MBTI? [Be aware that of the four dichotomies, this one is most observable in behavior and also the one most influenced by situational demands such as work environments or caring for children.]

2. When and in what situations do you typically use _____?
   (a Judging attitude or a Perceiving attitude—whichever the person prefers)

3. When and in what situations do you use _____? (the non-preferred pole)

If the preference is unclear after further discussion, ask:

4. Overall, when you are most able to do as you like, is it most satisfying and relaxing to operate with a plan or a schedule or to be free to do whatever appeals to you at the moment?

defined as an absence or deficit of the qualities that legitimately describe the other pole. For example, we might describe people who prefer Intuition as "imaginative." We would not then describe those who prefer Sensing as unimaginative, but rather as "pragmatic"—an alternative and qualitatively different focus of perception.

If questions remain after following the steps for clarifying a preference, the suggestions in Caution 4.2 and Don't Forget 4.1 may help.

A useful way to maintain adequate neutrality in explaining and verifying type, especially for an interpreter who is new to the system, is to have a variety of written explanatory materials available during the verification session. Depending on the nature of the materials, they can either be handed to the client or read aloud, adding material to suit the client's situation and one's own level of comfort and knowledge of the material. Interpreters can put together some explanatory materials on their own in addition to using various published aids for type verification. A variety of verification and interpretation resources that are geared to specific applications are available (see Kummerow, 1986; Lawrence & Martin, 1996; Myers, 1998).

### Step 3. Verify Each Preference

There are three situations that may occur during the verification process. First, the client may confirm the reported preference, spontaneously saying something like, "I know that one really fits me." Second, the client may identify the opposite preference to the one reported, for example, reporting a Feeling preference on the MBTI, but self-assessing a Thinking preference. Third, the client may express doubt about which pole of a dichotomy is preferred, saying something like, "On that one it could go either way," or "I think I answered about half and half." These three client reactions should be dealt with somewhat differently in relation to identifying best fit type.

*Self-assessed preference matches reported preference*   A simple statement such as "Yes, you answered indicating that you preferred _____" is sufficient. It is especially important here to help the client recognize that he or she also has access to and uses the less preferred pole of that dichotomy. The relevant queries in Rapid References 4.2 through 4.5 are helpful here. Then, depending on the client and context, you might move into a discussion of this particular preference in relation to the area of interest. For example,

"Can you describe a way that you use your Feeling preference in your work as a manager?" Or, if your client is a couple, "Are there times when your opposite preferences on Extraversion and Introversion create some difficulties for you?"

*Self-assessed preference is different from reported preference*    This response is often, though not always, associated with a slight or moderate preference clarity category. You will recall from Chapter 3 that both the preference clarity index, which is a number ranging from 1 to 30, and the preference clarity category, which is designated as "slight," "moderate," "clear," or "very clear," are estimates of the degree of confidence that the preference has been correctly identified. Regardless of reported clarity, you might say something like, "On that one you answered indicating you preferred the opposite one, so it would be a good idea for you to read the two different type descriptions that might apply."

*Client does not identify a preference*    If the reported type is associated with a slight or even moderate preference clarity, you can say something like, "Yes. It's hard to tell which one you prefer. I'll ask you to read the two different type descriptions that may apply. Perhaps one will fit you better than the other."

When discussing self-assessment that differs from reported type, it is important to avoid conveying that the client "guessed wrong" or lacks self-awareness. Discrepancies between reported and self-assessed type are more easily attributable to the way the interpreter described the poles and/or "social desirability" assumptions on the client's part—for example, believing that Thinking judgment is superior to Feeling judgment. Often, but not always, a client's self-assessment is reflected in his or her reported clarity of preference. Clients who quickly identify their preference are likely to have a clear or very clear preference clarity category. Clients who are unsure about a preference, or pick the opposite one to what they reported on the MBTI, may have a slight preference clarity category. However, reported preference clarity and *experienced* preference clarity are not always the same: Someone reporting a slight preference may experience the preference quite clearly and readily confirm it during verification. At times a moderate or clearly reported preference may be associated with some experienced doubt or even a self-assessment favoring the pole opposite to the one reported. Note that clarity of *reported* preference is entirely a function of the consistency with which a respondent has answered in choosing one pole of the dichotomy over the other. Consistently choosing one pole does not imply inability to use its op-

posite, nor does less consistency in answering imply ambivalence, lack of differentiation, or equal facility with two opposite poles.

Bear in mind that each dichotomy is complex and multifaceted, with
identifiable, though interrelated, component parts. The extended form of the
Indicator, which yields the profile and *MBTI Step II Expanded Interpretive Report*
(Quenk & Kummerow, 1996) elicits information about an individual's use of
some of these components. Slight and moderate preference clarity may result
from habitual or situational use of one or more components of the pole of a
dichotomy that is opposite to the underlying preference. For example, someone who prefers Intuition may habitually show a "Realistic" approach when
perceiving (the Sensing component) rather than an "Imaginative" approach
(the Intuitive component).

Step II information is not necessary for effective verification and interpretation of the MBTI; however, it is helpful to be aware that there are normal
and expected variations in expression of preferences that relate to differential
use of the components of each dichotomy. Keeping this in mind can discourage unjustified assumptions about the meaning of reported preference
clarity.

Caution 4.2 covers alternative meanings of "slight," "moderate," "clear,"
and "very clear" preferences and suggests lines of inquiry to follow that take
differential use of dichotomy components into account. How extensively one
should explore the possible meaning of clarity of preference with a particular
client is an individual judgment. Determining best fit type may be more relevant at a later time, perhaps as type is applied to a particular issue of interest
to the client.

### Step 4. Verify Best Fit Type

Depending on which format of the Indicator you administered, there are several options for identifying the client's best fit type. At this point in the verification process, one or more of the 16 types will be under consideration.
These will include the type that was reported—which will often be the same
as self-assessed type—and one or more other types, depending on which dichotomies were in question for the particular client. If you used a format that
produces a computer-generated report and type description, you can ask the
client to read that type description. If such a report is not available and/or
the client needs to consider alternative types to the one described in his or her

# CAUTION

## 4.2 Meaning of Clarity of Reported Preference and Suggested Lines of Inquiry

| | |
|---|---|
| Very clear | Usually affirms the preference and identifies with most of the qualities associated with it. A very clear preference results from answering most questions favoring one pole; it does not mean the person never uses the other member of the pair. *Make sure to ask about how and when the opposite pole is used.* |
| Clear | Likely to affirm the preference and identify with many of the qualities associated with it; may offer instances when uses opposite pole. There may be habitual or situational use of one *component* of the opposite pole. *Inquire about situations that may stimulate use of opposite function or attitude.* |
| Moderate | Usually agrees with preference but may express some doubt; and/or, may describe consistent use of some aspects of the opposite; or may identify opposite as better fit, and describe consistent use of some aspects of the reported preference. There may be habitual or situational use of one or two *components* of the opposite pole. *Inquire about which aspects of both poles are used and whether varying circumstances are related to such use.* |
| Slight | May affirm preference but readily mention aspects of the opposite that are used habitually—especially in particular situations; or may find the opposite fits better overall and mention aspects of reported preference that are used habitually; or may not be able to identify a preference. There may be habitual or situational use of one or more *components* of the opposite pole. *Spend more time exploring typical uses of both poles, the influence of situational factors, and satisfaction and dissatisfaction with such uses.* |

report, the 16 type descriptions in the booklet *Introduction to Type* (Myers, 1998) should be used. Regardless of the scoring method—computer profile, computer report, one of the template methods, or (in the case of larger groups) the self-scorable version—each client must have access to comprehensive descriptions of all 16 types. The descriptions in *Introduction to Type* are the most complete and well-validated available. The information in the other specialized introductions to type can also aid verification. These resources are particularly effective when interpreting the MBTI in relation to a particular area of application. Application areas covered are type and selling (Brock, 1994), type in college (DiTiberio & Hammer, 1993), type and careers (Hammer, 1993), type and teams (Hirsh, 1992), and type and organizations (Hirsh & Kummerow, 1998).

It is highly recommended that every client leave the verification and interpretation experience with a personal copy of *Introduction to Type* (Myers, 1998). Practitioner experience strongly suggests that clients who receive only their own type description with little explanatory information are much less likely to use the information productively than those who have access to all 16 descriptions.

Before you have a client read a type description, regardless of whether or not there is agreement with the reported type, explain that no type description will fit a person exactly or in all respects. If best fit type is in doubt, have the client read the type description that corresponds to reported type *first*. Ask the client to make note of and tell you which, if any, parts of the description do not fit. Usually, these will reflect the preference or preferences that are in doubt. If more than one alternative type must be explored, the client's comments can help you decide which type description should be read next. For the majority of clients, reading one alternative type description is all that is necessary. Most people find themselves well described or at least better described in one of the 16 type descriptions.

### Step 5. Using Type Dynamics in the Verification Process

It is important for clients to know that their personality type does not restrict them or categorize them in some stereotypical way. The best way to discourage such notions is to include a discussion of type dynamics—the hierarchy of comfort is the use of dominant, auxiliary, tertiary, and inferior functions and the attitudes of Extraversion or Introversion in which they are typically expressed. Sometimes exploring one or another aspect of type dynamics with a client can clarify one or more preferences.

Suppose, for example, that a client has verified S, F, and J but remains unsure about E or I. She has read the type descriptions for ESFJ and ISFJ and finds them about equally applicable. We know from our discussion of type dynamics in Chapter 1 that an ESFJ has dominant extraverted Feeling, auxiliary Introverted Sensing, tertiary Intuition, and inferior introverted Thinking; an ISFJ, in contrast, has dominant introverted Sensing, auxiliary extraverted

Feeling, tertiary Thinking, and inferior extraverted Intuition. Among other things, we would expect some differences between these two types in how they typically react to stress: An ESFJ's inferior introverted Thinking may come out as uncharacteristic, harsh criticism of others whereas an ISFJ's inferior extraverted Intuition is likely to emerge as negativism and catastrophizing about the future. Chapter 6 includes brief information about type and stress reactions for each of the types.

When appropriate, clients can also be directed to the one-page summary of type dynamics and development that is included in *Introduction to Type* (Myers, 1998, p. 35). Other resources can provide a practical knowledge about specific dynamic and developmental differences among the types too (see Corlett & Millner, 1993; Myers & Kirby, 1994; Quenk, 1993, 1996). Many helpful sources are included in the annotated bibliography that concludes this book.

## Verifying Type With Couples, Families, and Groups

The steps described above are geared to an individual interpretation, but the same guidelines and procedures can be easily adapted for use in a joint verification with couples or families, as well as with larger groups brought together for a particular reason. Issues relevant to verification and interpretation of type for couples and families are often embedded in clinical application of the MBTI and are therefore more fully discussed in Chapter 6.

## Cautions When Verifying Type With Particular Kinds of Clients

A verification session need not result in a client settling on a best fit type, and it is important that the client feel comfortable and affirmed despite any doubts that remain. These doubts can best be framed as interesting areas for self-observation and further exploration. Be aware, however, that not coming to closure about type can be more frustrating for some types than for others —most notably people who have a Judging preference on the J–P dichotomy. Such clients may be more willing to tolerate a period of self-exploration if a time limit on the process is suggested.

## Age of Client

The developmental nature of type leads to an expectation that younger people, older people, and people undergoing a significant life transition may have difficulty verifying a type. Young people in particular may be unclear on several dichotomies, and if identifying a preference is an issue for them, they should be told that "trying out" different ways of being is both common and can be helpful for people their age. Like any developmental area, there is wide variation in the age at which the type of a child or adolescent may be clear. Some children are very clear about their preferences. That a child's type is clear at an early age, however, does not mean that it is necessarily well developed. "One-sided" use of type is natural in children, and it may be useful to check out whether they are giving adequate attention to the "opposite" sides of themselves. Type "exaggeration" can be even more extreme in adolescents as they go about trying to establish a comfortable identity.

People of advancing years may have incorporated the less preferred aspects of their personality to some extent, and this may result in less clear preferences in answering the MBTI, experientially, or both. Older people can sometimes identify their natural type most readily by reflecting on how they were during the part of their adulthood when they were both most active as well as most free to be themselves. Verifying type for older people can be a less important goal than the understanding that often emerges through the process of considering type differences.

## Life Transitions

Any major life transition can contribute to doubts about oneself and a motivation to try new approaches. Adolescence and midlife represent such transitions for most people. In addition, such events as a major career change, marriage, divorce, death of spouse, retirement, may affect both how people answer the Indicator as well as how they assess their type. Some individuals actually recognize their natural type for the first time during a major transitional period. For others, a change in personal circumstances can lead to awareness of unknown talents and competencies in using the less preferred parts of themselves.

*Pathology*

As mentioned in Chapter 2, moderate to severe pathology, including active chemical addiction, can impair a client's ability to report on and verify natural type. Type verification with such clients may be secondary to a specific therapeutic goal. It is advisable not to dwell on complete verification when giving MBTI results to such clients, focusing instead on the purpose for which it was administered. Information about appropriate uses of the MBTI with disturbed clients is included in Chapter 6.

Before moving on to the interpretation section of this chapter, it will be helpful to keep in mind the characteristics of the MBTI that lead to some of its psychometric qualities and also necessitate verification of results by the client. Don't Forget 4.2 summarizes these characteristics.

## TYPE INTERPRETATION

Type verification and type interpretation are interrelated aspects of a single enterprise. An effective interpreter uses illustrations relevant to the area of in-

---

## DON'T FORGET

### 4.2 MBTI Characteristics Underlying Its Psychometric Properties

- Based on Jung's theory of psychological types
- Postulates dichotomous opposites, not continua
- Postulates qualitatively different types, not universal traits
- Specifies theory-driven dynamic interactions among preferences
- Four scales designed to be psychometrically independent
- Moderate, theoretically justified correlation between S–N and J–P scales
- 93 items in forced-choice item format; two choices per item
- Two kinds of items: phrase questions and word pairs
- Items selected and scored using item response theory
- Items worded for comparable attractiveness
- No significant gender or age differences
- Tied points are designated I, N, F, P
- Omissions allowed

terest as an aid in verification, and clients often discover practical ways to apply type during the process of identifying their best fit type. For example, in verifying type with a couple, examples or experiences will emerge that confirm type preferences and also shed light on their communication problems, kinds of arguments, problems with child rearing, or whatever issues led them to seek help.

## Reasons for Taking the MBTI

People take the MBTI for a wide variety of reasons: because of personal curiosity, for career exploration or other work-related purpose, during couple therapy or personal therapy, in a chemical addiction treatment program. Regardless of the issue involved, an overriding goal is to assess individuals from the vantage point of their own type. A type framework views strengths as resulting from practicing and refining natural preferences and weaknesses as the concomitant of devoting less time and energy to nonpreferred mental functions and attitudes. Characteristics that may be seen as deficiencies or as "diagnostic" within a normative framework may be recognized as "normal" and adaptive for a person of that type. Similarly, a person whose behavior deviates markedly from what is typical for his or her type may actually be experiencing significant psychological difficulties. For example, it is not surprising for an ISFP to judge himself as less competent and effective than is justified by objective criteria, whereas such self-doubt would be unusual and therefore a cause for concern in an INTJ.

There is a great deal of information available about type in relation to teaching and learning styles; career choices; use of psychological services and attraction to different therapeutic approaches; management and leadership styles; how different types typically communicate, resolve conflict, cope with stress—and many more useful ways of understanding differences as a function of personality type. Information about these and other variables is available in the MBTI manual (Myers et al., 1998) and in other publications. These resources provide interpreters with important background information and a framework for understanding individual clients. In addition, the type verification process itself often permits the interpreter to discover important ways that an individual differs from what is typical for that type. For example, a particular ISFP may express a great deal of self-confidence, having had many significant validating experiences; the INTJ who devalues himself may reveal that his Intuition was systematically discounted and ridiculed when he was growing up. Awareness of the impact of environmental pressures on natural type will discourage a simplistic and stereotypical interpretation of MBTI results. When a client has verified a type but does not seem like that type, exploring the reasons for the "aberration" can be enlightening.

Interpreters of the MBTI must also be wary of simplistic and incorrect uses of research data, particularly those showing type differences in such areas as career choice, managerial status, and leadership roles. A common error made by laypeople, professionals, and critics of the MBTI alike is to assume that the types who predominate in an endeavor are therefore more suited for it or "better" at it. In fact, type theory predicts that individuals of different types will be differentially *attracted* to different occupations and work characteristics such as managerial and leadership roles. The theory does not predict competence or satisfaction, nor is there any expectation or empirical evidence that a rare type in a position will be "unsuited for it," less competent, or less satisfied. Rather, he or she is likely to be different from the predominant type in terms of the way the job is done, particular motivations, nature of satisfactions, and the like. Caution 4.3 lists ways in which the MBTI should *not* be interpreted.

## Interpreting Type in a Clinical Setting

One needn't have a specific reason to give a client the MBTI beyond a desire to take type into account in assessment and subsequent treatment. Merely being aware of type differences enables the clinician to remain open to and curious about the individuality of each client, to suspend judgment, and to avoid a premature diagnosis. An aware clinician can more readily distinguish among client characteristics that reflect normal type preferences, those that may be related to the individual's type development, those that reveal a person's distinctive way of expressing type, and those that are independent of type considerations.

### Using Type "Language" in Interpretation

There are a variety of situations in which the results of a type assessment must be communicated to someone who knows little or nothing about type, for example as part of a written report in assessments for treatment or in employee assessment. The interpreter's task is not to educate recipients of such reports about type or the MBTI but rather to provide useful information *without* using type terminology. This is especially true since type language can easily be relegated to the category of "psychological jargon" and summarily dismissed.

Knowing when and how to modify one's language style as an interpreter is one very effective use of type, and it is relevant in a broad range of therapeutic and other endeavors in addition to explaining MBTI results. Even when introducing type terms during a verification session, care should be taken not to overload clients with more terms than are necessary for adequate understanding. On the other hand, some clients (often those who prefer either Sensing and/or Thinking) appreciate precise terminology and find results less credible when "technical" terms are omitted from an explanation. The kind of language clients prefer is often related to their typological makeup in combination with their educational and occupational background.

### Type Distributions as an Interpretive Aid

Familiarity with the characteristics of the 16 types promotes recognition of expected type-related behavior. It can also be helpful to know the prevalence of the types in the general population and in particular environments. Some client concerns may be related to being a type that is infrequent in the population at large or in a particular setting. For example, only about 25% of the U.S. population prefer Intuition over Sensing, with INFJ least frequent among males (1.2%) and ISTJ (16.4%) the most frequent; INTJ are the least frequent among females (.9%) and ISFJ (19.4%) the most frequent. When a

**Table 4.1    Type Distribution of the National Representative Sample**

|  | ISTJ | | ISFJ | | INFJ | | INTJ | |
|---|---|---|---|---|---|---|---|---|
|  | $N$ | % | $N$ | % | $N$ | % | $N$ | % |
| Male[a] | 242 | 16.4 | 119 | 8.1 | 19 | 1.2 | 49 | 3.3 |
| Female[b] | 106 | 6.9 | 297 | 19.4 | 25 | 1.6 | 13 | 0.9 |
| Total population[c] | 348 | 11.6 | 416 | 13.8 | 44 | 1.5 | 62 | 2.1 |

|  | ISTP | | ISFP | | INFP | | INTP | |
|---|---|---|---|---|---|---|---|---|
|  | $N$ | % | $N$ | % | $N$ | % | $N$ | % |
| Male[a] | 126 | 8.5 | 112 | 7.6 | 61 | 4.1 | 71 | 4.8 |
| Female[b] | 36 | 2.3 | 152 | 9.9 | 71 | 4.6 | 27 | 1.7 |
| Total population[c] | 162 | 5.4 | 264 | 8.8 | 132 | 4.4 | 98 | 3.3 |

|  | ESTP | | ESFP | | ENFP | | ENTP | |
|---|---|---|---|---|---|---|---|---|
|  | $N$ | % | $N$ | % | $N$ | % | $N$ | % |
| Male[a] | 83 | 5.6 | 102 | 6.9 | 95 | 6.4 | 59 | 4.0 |
| Female[b] | 46 | 3.0 | 153 | 10.1 | 148 | 9.7 | 37 | 2.4 |
| Total population[c] | 129 | 4.3 | 256 | 8.5 | 243 | 8.1 | 96 | 3.2 |

|  | ESTJ | | ESFJ | | ENFJ | | ENTJ | |
|---|---|---|---|---|---|---|---|---|
|  | $N$ | % | $N$ | % | $N$ | % | $N$ | % |
| Male[a] | 165 | 11.2 | 111 | 7.5 | 24 | 1.6 | 40 | 2.7 |
| Female[b] | 96 | 6.3 | 259 | 16.9 | 50 | 3.3 | 14 | 0.9 |
| Total population[c] | 261 | 8.7 | 369 | 12.3 | 74 | 2.5 | 54 | 1.8 |

*Note.* From Myers et al. (1998, p. 298). Modified and reproduced by special permission of the Publisher, Consulting Psychologists Press, Inc., Palo Alto, CA 94303 from *MBTI® Manual: A Guide to the Development and Use of the Myers-Briggs Type Indicator,* Third Edition by Isabel Briggs Myers, Mary H. McCaulley, Naomi L. Quenk, and Allen L. Hammer. Copyright 1998 by Consulting Psychologists Press, Inc. All rights reserved. Further reproduction is prohibited without the Publisher's written consent. [a]$N$ = 1,478. [b]$N$ = 1,531. [c]$N$ = 3,009.

person of a more rare type reports feeling different, like an outsider, or misunderstood, it may be helpful to validate that perception with statistics.

Table 4.1 gives the type distribution for the national representative sample of U.S. adults as reported in Myers, McCaulley, Quenk, and Hammer (1998). Stratified random sampling representative of the U.S. population was used in collecting a national sample, followed by weighting based on U.S. census data for gender and ethnicity, which corrected for an overrepresentation of Caucasian females and an underrepresentation of African Americans males in the national sample. The information on type distributions can be quite useful in clinical and other applications and is also the best available general sample to use as a base comparison group in research. See Myers, McCaulley, Quenk, and Hammer (1998) for type distributions in different ethnic groups that are based on the national representative sample, as well as distributions of type in a number of different countries.

Type prevalence can also be helpful at a more personal level, such as when a client becomes aware of the likely types of family members or of colleagues at work. For example, a woman with a Sensing preference who was raised in a family of Intuitive types may end up feeling less intellectually swift and imaginative than her parents and siblings; an ESFJ working among ISFJs and ISTJs may believe he lacks the requisite ability to concentrate and persevere silently until a task is completed; an INFP engineer may worry that his performance is poor because his primarily Thinking supervisors rarely compliment him but are quick to point out his mistakes.

Awareness of some general societal biases toward particular preferences or whole types can also be helpful in understanding and helping a client cope with specific issues. For example, many Introverts struggle with such labels as "shy," "unsociable," "cold," or "uncommunicative." Even though the national representative sample indicates about an equal frequency of people reporting a preference for Extraversion and those preferring Introversion, our culture in general clearly favors extraverted qualities over introverted ones. It should be noted that many earlier estimates of the prevalence of Extraversion and Introversion in the United States suggested that there were three to four times as many Extraverts as Introverts. These estimates were based on various samples that were not representative of the population at large, such as Myers and McCaulley's (1985) high school student sample.

Another source of bias comes from gender expectations, particularly in confusing Thinking judgment with masculinity and Feeling judgment with femininity—exacerbated by mistakenly defining Thinking as hard-headed or unfeeling and Feeling as emotional. A lesser expectation is that women are by nature extraverted and men introverted. In fact, the T–F dichotomy is the only one of the four that has consistently shown a gender difference in prevalence. In the national representative sample, about 57% of men identify Thinking and 43% Feeling as their preference; about 25% of women identify Thinking and 75% Feeling as their preference. It is interesting that compared with earlier, less carefully drawn samples, a greater percentage of *both* men and women identify Feeling as their preference. Also in contrast with earlier samples, slightly more women prefer Extraversion (52%) and somewhat more men prefer Introversion (54%). Regardless of actual prevalence in the population, it is important to differentiate natural preferences for Thinking or Feeling from legitimate gender differences and to help clients understand and evaluate the impact that a confusion of type and gender may have on their lives. For example, women who prefer Thinking and men who prefer Feeling are judged differently—and often negatively—relative to women who prefer Feeling and men who prefer Thinking. Another frequent error is the assumption that all women "should" be Feeling types and all men "should" be Thinking types. Men and women who deviate from this expectation can be seen as deficient in masculinity and femininity when the distinctive qualities of the two judging functions are mistakenly fused and confused with gender qualities.

### *Biases and Expectations Associated With Type Preferences*
Regardless of whether a type bias is societal, context driven, or based on one's own type, awareness of some of the assumptions that influence our perception of type-related characteristics can be helpful when assessing and treating clients of different types. As a general rule, we assume that other people's minds operate in much the same way as our own and that to understand the meaning and motivation behind other's words and actions, we must simply consider what *we* would mean and what *our* motivation would be in the same situation.

This reasonable but incorrect assumption is the basis for much interpersonal misunderstanding. The type perspective provides a practical way of interpreting or "translating" the words and actions of people with different type perspectives. Clinicians can use this information in helping clients better understand themselves and others, as well as to accommodate client differences in their conduct of psychotherapy and in the expectations they have of clients.

## Maturity and Expression of Type

The type descriptions in *Introduction to Type* (Myers, 1998) represent mature, well-developed members of each type. Many individuals, including most young people, may not fit the descriptions. They may show exaggerations of some of the characteristics described, lack others, or appear to be caricatures of their type. When an adult comes across as a caricature—sharpening all of the qualities of the type so they come across as rigid and extreme—they are often seen as immature. A seeming paradox is that people whose expression of type is developed and mature may appear to be less obviously their type than those who are more immature in their development.

### *An Example*

At age 10, Billy was referred for treatment because of his difficulty controlling his temper and for his impatience, outspoken criticism, and rudeness toward his parents and teachers. His failing grades in school were primarily due to incomplete or sloppily done assignments rather than to his cognitive abilities, which were judged to be superior. Billy showed quite a lot of creativity and originality in explaining the reasons for what others saw as his problems, essentially blaming people and external circumstances for what happened. His current teacher suggested that he might be hyperactive; his parents wondered if his self-centeredness was due to his being an only and much catered to child. Because of his age, Billy took the Murphy-Meisgeier Type Indicator for Children, with results suggesting his type was ESFP, although his scores were close to the "undecided" range on the S–N and T–F dichotomies. On this children's type indicator, a "U-Band" identifies a range of scores called "Undecided," acknowledging the assumption that type preferences develop and become clear over time. Indeed, Billy's behavior did fit expectations for an immature Extraverted Perceiving type (one whose dominant function is either S or N and is habitually used in the Extraverted attitude). Behavior that might reflect an S or N preference was ambiguous: He excelled at memorizing facts about geography, which he loved, but was haphazard at best in remembering most other details. He was quick to come up with original solutions to math problems but disdainful of having to record the steps to solutions. With regard to Thinking and Feeling, research shows that a reported Feeling preference predominates among children and that a preference for Thinking may not be verified until later years. The ongoing research of Elizabeth Murphy, coauthor of the Murphy-Meisgeier inventory, indicates that a Thinking preference in young children is primarily shown through being independent (Murphy, 1998). An immature way of expressing a Feeling preference is to focus on one's own well-being and emotions with little regard for the impact one has on the values and well-being of others. Billy's reported slight preference for Feeling perhaps came out immaturely in frequent accusations that others were "hurting my feelings." In addition, and from a dynamic perspective, Billy's expression of Feeling as "raw emotion" is reminiscent of Feeling expressed as the inferior function of dominant Thinking types (Quenk, 1993, 1996).

Billy's behavior and attitude problems diminished considerably after a year of individual and family therapy. His behavior was interpreted in terms of the intense "pull" he experienced both from and toward the environment, his desire for and attraction to external stimulation, and the accompanying ease with which Billy became distracted. Ways of helping Billy capitalize on his type preferences rather than change them were found. He was helped to accomplish tasks by making use of his high energy and keen awareness of what was going on, while gradually developing self-discipline and the ability to gauge how long tasks would take and how to better meet deadlines.

Billy fared reasonably well over the next several years, with infrequent lapses into his former problematical behavior. However, at age 14 he returned for therapy due to failing grades in several middle school subjects—again ascribed to incomplete and sloppy assignments and work that was not handed in. Billy's excuse-making abilities had become more sophisticated and even more original and clever than they were at age 10. Billy took the MBTI Form

G (Form M was not yet published), was able to answer all but two questions, and came out as an ENTP with very clear preferences for E, N and P, and a moderate preference for T. Note that as mentioned earlier, neither the clarity of Billy's reported preferences nor his verifying of them necessarily reflect effective and mature expression of his type.

A standard verification procedure was followed, with Billy verifying all four preferences, but with some doubts about the Sensing–Intuition dichotomy. Billy read the type description in *Introduction to Type* (Myers, 1998) aloud to his therapist and parents. All agreed that most of the descriptive statements fit Billy. For example, he was certainly "creative, imaginative, and clever; analytical, logical, rational, and [questionably] objective," and, though often inappropriately, he was indeed "assertive and questioning." Most striking, however, were the statements describing ENTPs who are not using their type in a mature fashion. These ENTPs were described as "brash, rude, and abrasive, given to criticizing others, becoming rebellious and combative, scattered and unable to focus." Even Billy laughed at the obvious accuracy of these descriptors.

Both Billy and his parents were assured that Billy was in the process of "growing into his type" and that working with this information would continue to be helpful in his genuine desire to meet other's expectations while remaining true to his own nature. Billy's parents had taken the MBTI during Billy's earlier therapy, and Billy read their type descriptions to better understand their concerns about him and what he could do to accommodate their needs as well as his own.

Billy's therapy was a unique opportunity to observe an emerging, though immature, type and to explore ways that type knowledge could be used effectively over the course of psychotherapy.

## Interpretation Issues and Stability of Type Over Time

The Jung/Myers theory postulates that every individual is born with a natural disposition to develop certain attitudes and mental processes rather than their opposites. An important related assumption is that one's type remains stable throughout life, although the way it is expressed at different developmental stages can differ. Innate type develops and becomes individualized or derailed—in response to a variety of life experiences and environmental pressures, some of which were suggested in the preceding sections. There are two effects of developmental and interactional influences that relate to the stability of type over time. The first may be elicited during the verification and interpretation procedure; the second is reflected in reliability evidence.

### Client Belief That Type Changes

Some clients believe that their type was different at an earlier time and has changed (e.g., "I used to be an Introvert but now I'm an Extravert"). If the client is referring only to his reported MBTI results—he took the MBTI a few years ago, came out as an Introvert and has taken it again and reported Extraversion as his preference—the interpreter can correct the client's notion that a change in reported preference represents an actual personality change. If, however, the client means that he experienced himself and behaved previously like an Introvert and is now operating as an Extravert, inquiry should be made into which pole of the Extraversion–Introversion dichotomy is really natural for him. A consideration of some of the issues discussed earlier in this chapter might be productive in this exploration.

### Test-Retest Reliability

Results for people who retake the Indicator after an interval of time may also be affected by the various developmental and interactional factors discussed. Most samples for whom reliability data are available contain a range of ages and intellectual achievement, both factors that appear to affect consistency of response on the MBTI. Therefore reliability results in general are probably low estimates of what might be obtained with more select samples. With longer time intervals, some changes in self-report may occur as a result of increased self-knowledge, better comprehension of questions, and so on.

Table 4.2 gives the test-retest reliabilities for available Form M samples using the percentage of respondents who remained the same on one to four categories on retest. For Form M using three different samples, results for Consulting Psychologists Press employees (employees of the publisher who likely had some familiarity with type) are best, and the college student sample are least consistent in having all four categories the same. Reliability for

**Table 4.2    Percentage of Individuals Remaining the Same on One to Four Categories on Retest**

| Sample | Interval | $N$ | 4 | 3 | 2 | 1 | 0 |
|---|---|---|---|---|---|---|---|
| *Form M* | | | | | | | |
| Students | 4 weeks | 116 | 55 | 93 | 97 | 100 | 0 |
| Utility adults | 4 weeks | 258 | 66 | 91 | 99 | 100 | 0 |
| Consulting Psychologists Press | 4 weeks | 50 | 80 | 100 | | | |
| *Form G* | | | | | | | |
| Meta-analysis | >9 months | 559 | 36 | 72 | 94 | 100 | 0 |
| Meta-analysis | <9 months | 1,139 | 51 | 87 | 98 | 100 | 0 |

Header spanning columns 4–0: **Number of Preferences the Same at Retest**

longer intervals is provided in a meta-analysis of Form G subjects. Even here, results are acceptable, given the length of the intervals.

**The Ethics of Verification and Interpretation**

As is the case for administration of the MBTI, standard ethical guidelines for tests apply to interpretation of the MBTI. In addition, because results are designed to be given directly to the respondent, some other considerations also

# DON'T FORGET

## 4.3 Ethical Guidelines Regarding Interpretation of MBTI Results

### Principle 11. Guidelines for Interpretation of Results

Both the letter and the spirit of psychological type theory, as oriented toward the appreciation and positive utilization of individual differences, should characterize the interpretation of type results to individuals and groups.

1. Type attributes should be described in non-judgmental or positive terms and as tendencies rather than imperatives. Words like "preference," "tendency," and "inclination" are consistent with psychological type theory. Explicit reference should be made to the inherent value of all types.

2. Respondents should be informed that psychological type theory reflects an individual's preferences, and not abilities, intelligence, or likelihood of success. Consequently, the practitioner should not counsel a person toward or away from a particular career, activity, or personal relationship, based solely upon type information.

3. The individual receiving type results is considered the judge of whether the type description "fits" or not. Where the individual disagrees with the description associated with reported scores, the practitioner should help the person identify the most suitable type description.

4. In providing information about psychological type theory to individuals and groups, care should be taken not to state or imply that type explains everything, but rather that it is one important component of very complex human personalities.

5. Interpreters of psychological type theory should be sensitive to their own type biases. They should exert every effort not to communicate type biases to respondents.

6. Practitioners should interpret type information within the limits of currently available knowledge. They should be careful not to make inferences regarding type or the scores on any type indicator that go beyond data.

7. Practitioners should not use psychological type indicators whose reliability and validity have not been demonstrated, or use parts of demonstrably reliable and valid type indicators unless the parts themselves have been demonstrated to be reliable and valid.

*Note.* From "Ethical Principles," Association for Psychological Type (1992, pp. 4, 5). Used with permission.

apply. Don't Forget 4.3 summarizes them, as described in the Association for Psychological Type's "Ethical Principles" (1992).

## Computerized Interpretive Reports

Several computerized narrative reports are produced through the computer-scoring options for the MBTI. Rapid Reference 4.5 describes them and gives the associated Consulting Psychologists Press product numbers for ease in ordering the forms that will produce these reports.

### ≡ Rapid Reference

#### 4.5 Selected MBTI Profiles and Reports

| Profile/Report | Description |
| --- | --- |
| Prepaid Profile: 6188-M116 | Basic preference information in a two-page report |
| Prepaid Interpretive Report: 6132-M116 | Profile and type description of reported type in a four-page report |
| Prepaid Interpretive Report for Organizations: 6138-M116 | Ten-page profile and report that focuses on the individual's type as it is expressed in business and organizational settings |
| Prepaid Career Report 6153-M116 | Seven-page report linking client type with career information and strategies for improving job satisfaction |
| Prepaid Strong & MBTI Career Report 8673-11018 | Strong Interest Inventory and MBTI results integrated for the client to identify occupations in a comprehensive career development system. A 10-page report. |
| Individual Report Form 6134-M116 | A form for recording results when using the template-scored version. Gives brief definitions of preferences, space to record results, and one page of thumbnail descriptions of the 16 types. |

**Basic Psychometric Evidence**

This chapter has suggested various guidelines for verifying and interpreting the MBTI, as well as a number of caveats that take into account the factors that can limit the accuracy with which the MBTI can elicit and identify a particular individual's type. Practitioners can also make effective use of basic psychometric information for the MBTI, both for their own confidence and understanding as well as to answer questions that clients may ask about the likelihood that the MBTI can tell them something important about themselves. To facilitate these goals, Table 4.3 summarizes this information. Note that the test-retest reliability data in Table 4.3 can be particularly helpful when clients report coming out as a different type on a previous or subsequent administration of the MBTI. One likely explanation is the clarity with which they reported their preferences on the two administrations. The data show that reliabilities on retest for people

**Table 4.3   Summary of Selected Psychometric Evidence**

| Internal Consistency Reliabilities | | | E–I | S–N | T–F | J–P |
|---|---|---|---|---|---|---|
| (Coefficient alpha) | 1,330 males | | .91 | .93 | .90 | .93 |
| Form M | 1,529 females | | .90 | .93 | .88 | .92 |
| | 7 combined samples (500 males and females) | | .94 | .93 | .92 | .93 |

| Test-Retest Reliabilities | Preference Clarity Index | N | E–I | S–N | T–F | J–P |
|---|---|---|---|---|---|---|
| Form M theta scores | 1–5 | 88 | .46 | .52 | .44 | .22 |
| by preference clarity | 6–10 | 78 | .83 | .72 | .73 | .75 |
| index ranges for 7 | 11–15 | 62 | .87 | .87 | .84 | .89 |
| samples combined | 16–20 | 62 | .90 | .88 | .90 | .93 |
| ($N$=500) | 21–25 | 64 | .97 | .96 | .95 | .93 |
| | 26–30 | 70 | .99 | .99 | .99 | .99 |

**Table 4.3    continued**

| | |
|---|---|
| Validity of E–I | Correlates with other measures of Extraversion, and in the expected directions with at least 157 other relevant variables |
| Validity of S–N | Correlates in the expected directions with at least 126 other relevant variables |
| Validity of T–F | Correlates in the expected directions with at least 97 other relevant variables |
| Validity of J–P | Correlates in the expected directions with at least 84 other relevant variables |
| Validity of whole types | Hundreds of type tables for different occupations showing distributions in accord with theoretical predictions; numerous studies by whole type, especially in Myers et al. (1998) |
| Validity of type dynamics | Dynamic analysis using observer ratings supports dynamic interpretation; ANOVA method that examined interactions specific to type dynamic groupings in national sample data found strong evidence in support of dynamic interactions. |

*Note.* For details on the nature of variables and size of correlations for E–I, S–N, T–F, and J–P, see Myers et al. (1998, pp. 175–184). For details on studies validating whole type and type dynamics, see Myers et al. (1998, pp. 203–218). Reliability figures from Myers et al. (1998, pp. 161, 163). Modified and reproduced by special permission of the Publisher, Consulting Psychologists Press, Inc., Palo Alto, CA 94303 from *MBTI® Manual: A Guide to the Development and Use of the Myers-Briggs Type Indicator,* Third Edition by Isabel Briggs Myers, Mary H. McCaulley, Naomi L. Quenk, and Allen L. Hammer. Copyright 1998 by Consulting Psychologists Press, Inc. All rights reserved. Further reproduction is prohibited without the Publisher's written consent.

with slight (preference clarity index 1–5) preference clarity are quite a bit lower than those for people with clear (preference clarity index 16–25) and very clear (preference clarity index 26–30) preference clarity. You can also tell clients who wonder if they would come out as a different type if they took the MBTI at a different time that there is strong evidence that they would come out the same, but if they came close to "splitting their votes" on a dichotomy, they could come out indicating the opposite preference on a second administration.

Similarly, clients who are interested in the meaningfulness of type dichotomies and how they relate to a variety of traits and other measures, can be told of the many relationships that have been found for each dichotomy. It is useful for an interpreter to be familiar with the kinds of variables that have been studied and to have access to data in which particular clients may be interested. Clients are even more likely to ask about whole types (e.g., "Which types are most compatible?" or "What kind of work do ISFJs like to do?"). Keeping a copy of the MBTI manual on hand is the best way to answer these kinds of specific client questions.

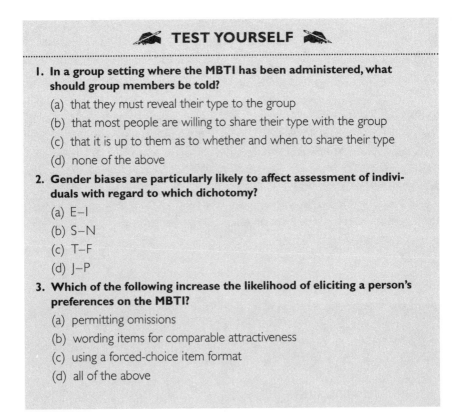

### 🖋 TEST YOURSELF 🖋

1. **In a group setting where the MBTI has been administered, what should group members be told?**
   (a) that they must reveal their type to the group
   (b) that most people are willing to share their type with the group
   (c) that it is up to them as to whether and when to share their type
   (d) none of the above

2. **Gender biases are particularly likely to affect assessment of individuals with regard to which dichotomy?**
   (a) E–I
   (b) S–N
   (c) T–F
   (d) J–P

3. **Which of the following increase the likelihood of eliciting a person's preferences on the MBTI?**
   (a) permitting omissions
   (b) wording items for comparable attractiveness
   (c) using a forced-choice item format
   (d) all of the above

4. **The four categories of preference clarity shown in the preference clarity category are "very clear," "clear," "moderate," and "slight."** True or False?

5. **People who have a low preference clarity index nearly always have difficulty identifying a preference.** True or False?

6. **The application of objective criteria is characteristic of**

   (a) Sensing types.

   (b) Thinking types.

   (c) Introverts.

   (d) Judging types.

7. **As a reflection of their desire for harmony, which of the following is true of Feeling types?**

   (a) They avoid confrontations.

   (b) They often accommodate other's desires.

   (c) They may make decisions that are not in accord with logic.

   (d) all of the above

8. **Every client must leave the verification session with a clear sense of his or her type.** True or False?

9. **Comfort working within a predetermined schedule is associated with a preference for**

   (a) Introversion.

   (b) Sensing.

   (c) Thinking.

   (d) Judging.

10. **The MBTI can be appropriately used to assess**

    (a) personality preferences.

    (b) competencies.

    (c) personality disorders.

    (d) the compatibility of a couple.

11. **Why is knowing one's own type important when verifying and interpreting type with clients?**

12. **What should you say to someone who believes that his type has changed?**

*continued*

13. There is little evidence that type predicts success in any career. Is this a valid criticism of the MBTI? Why or why not?

14. What might account for a person being characterized as "exaggerated" or a "caricature" of his or her type?

15. The MBTI treats Extraversion and Introversion as equally valid modes of energy. Yet Introverts are often labeled as "shy," a trait with negative connotations. How would you explain the difference between being introverted and being shy?

*Answers:* 1. c; 2. c; 3. d; 4. True; 5. False; 6. b; 7. d; 8. False; 9. d; 10. a; 11. It helps one recognize and avoid personal type biases; 12. More likely, you are *expressing* your type differently, but which type is natural for you could be further explored; 13. No, because the MBTI makes no claim for such a relationship; 14. Inadequate type development and/or habitual use of both dominant and auxiliary functions in the same attitude; 15. Shy people tend to be uncomfortable in social situations; Introverts tend to be adaptively energized by their inner life and may or may not be uncomfortable socially.

Five

# STRENGTHS AND WEAKNESSES OF THE MBTI

## OVERVIEW

Form M of the Myers-Briggs Type Indicator personality inventory was released in the fall of 1998 and has yet to be reviewed in major publications. There are a number of major differences between Form M and previous MBTI forms that can be assessed as advantages and disadvantages based on information in the 1998 revised test manual and some recent studies. Critical observations regarding some of the psychometric qualities of previous forms appear to have been successfully addressed in the Form M revision and revised manual. Critiques of these issues will therefore not be covered here, but relevant improvements are noted in appropriate Rapid References. Interested readers will find references to the sources of earlier critiques at the conclusion of this chapter.

There are several of general features of the MBTI that are largely independent of the form used. These will be considered first, followed by a review of the advantages and disadvantages of Form M relative to previous forms with regard to its development, administration and scoring, reliability and validity, standardization, and interpretation.

### The MBTI as a Personality Assessment Tool

Many of the qualities that can be seen as strengths of the MBTI also represent possible weaknesses. Rapid Reference 5.1 contrasts these.

### Strengths and Weaknesses of MBTI Form M

The MBTI revision process appears to have produced a psychometrically stronger instrument with few serious weaknesses. Improvement in the test it-

## 5.1 Strengths and Weaknesses of the MBTI

### Strengths

- The comprehensive theory provides a context for understanding individual complexity.
- Clients recognize the types as real and the typology as a useful way of describing themselves and others.
- Nonnormative basis of preferences and types identifies and affirms client individual differences as normal.
- Questions about simple surface behaviors adequately identify the complex constructs that interact, as specified in the theory.
- Test yields four largely psychometrically independent scales that are relatively unambiguous in what they measure.
- The test is parsimonious: It requires only four measured constructs to yield rich personality descriptions with broad applicability.

### Weaknesses

- Adequate understanding of the theory is needed to administer and interpret the instrument.
- Clients and professionals ascribe trait qualities to type preferences, leading to inappropriate interpretations of type.
- From a normative perspective, positive type descriptions too easily gloss over real psychological problems.
- Simplicity of questions encourages the idea that the typology itself is simple and static rather than complex and dynamic.
- The scales look like familiar trait measures, and can easily be interpreted as four independent traits.
- The 16 types are not measured directly; knowledge of theoretical assumptions regarding how the four scales interact dynamically is needed to identify types.

self is further supported by the quality of the third revision of the manual, which became available simultaneously with the publication of Form M. Strengths attributable to the manual are included as relevant points in Rapid References 5.2 through 5.6. It should be noted that some of the points included as weaknesses are not a function of the revision itself but are rather inevitable concomitants of introducing a major revision to an established instrument.

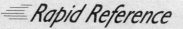

## 5.2 Strengths and Weakness of MBTI Form M Development

### Strengths

- Item response theory was used to evaluate and select the items that had the greatest discrimination around the midpoint of each scale.

- A large pool of items written by Myers formed the basis of the new form.

- A large pool of newly written items were evaluated, yielding nearly half of the selected items.

- Three-response items were revised so only two-option items are included.

- Items showing gender differences were eliminated, so no weighting for gender is required.

- Most items affected by respondent age were eliminated.

- Items showing any other differential item functioning (in addition to age and gender) were eliminated.

### Weaknesses

- Longtime users may resist giving up Myers's familiar prediction ratio method for item selection and scoring, which worked pretty well.

- Breadth of coverage of the multi-faceted content of the dichotomies may have been sacrificed in item selection.

- The moderate correlation between S and J, and between N and P appears to contradict the scale independence criterion; however, factor analyses of Form M clearly show S–N items loading on the S–N scale and J–P items loading on the J–P scale.

# Rapid Reference

## 5.3 Strengths and Weakness of MBTI Form M Administration and Scoring

### Strengths

- There are 93 items, all scored for type, one less than on Form G, which also contained an additional 32 research items.

- Item response theory, which is grounded in Modern Test Theory, is used for scoring, improving accuracy of results.

- Self-scorable form is easier to use than the self-scorable Form G.

- Test materials are visually attractive and instructions are clear and readily understandable.

- Four template scoring keys replace the former five keys.

- There are no weighted items, allowing quicker and more accurate template scoring.

### Weaknesses

- Different scoring options can produce different results, specifically template and self-scoring versus item response theory computer scoring.

- Differences among the scoring options are hard for users to understand.

- Researchers must have answer sheets computer scored to get the theta scores needed for correlational studies.

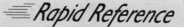
*Rapid Reference*

### 5.4 Strengths and Weakness of MBTI Form M Standardization

**Strengths**

- A stratified random sample was collected to match U.S. census data for adults 18 years of age and older.
- A weighted sample was created to approximate the U.S. distributions by gender and ethnicity, to produce a national representative sample.
- Reported distributions of preferences and types are more accurate than previous estimates and include distributions for African American, Asian American, and Latino/Latina ethnic groups.

**Weaknesses**

- The sample was slightly overrepresented with Caucasian females relative to U.S. census data and underrepresented for African American males.
- Desired representation in the stratified random sample would have been preferable to a weighted estimate.

# Rapid Reference

## 5.5 Strengths and Weakness of MBTI Form M Reliability and Validity

### Strengths

- There is improved internal consistency and test-retest reliabilities on all scales.
- There is improved accuracy relative to best fit type estimates.
- Manual validity information emphasizes research that studies the validity of whole types.
- Data presented throughout the manual provide strong support for type dynamics and the distinctiveness of the 16 types.

### Weaknesses

- Test-retest data are necessarily based on small samples and brief time periods.
- Larger samples to assess best fit type with Form M would be desirable.
- Research on the 16 whole types requires larger samples and an accurate understanding of the theory.
- Dynamics-oriented research techniques and results are more difficult to comprehend than simple correlational studies of the four dichotomies.
- The Form M database available for research is limited.

## 5.6 Strengths and Weakness of MBTI Form M Interpretation

### Strengths

- The term *preference clarity index* replaces the former term *preference score,* discouraging a trait interpretation of numbers.

- Language used in test instructions, profiles, and reports is consistent with a type rather than a trait approach.

- Test instructions and interpretation recommendations are consistent across all delivery formats.

- The term *dichotomy* is used rather than *scale* or *dimension* to refer to the MBTI's four categories; the term *scale* is restricted to psychometric issues; the term *dimension* is avoided entirely.

- The chapter on interpretation and the five application chapters in the manual provide practical, hands-on guidance to users in all areas of application.

### Weaknesses

- Longtime users may continue to use the term *score* and to think from a score perspective.

- It is sometimes awkward to use the term *dichotomy* rather than *scale;* MBTI dichotomies look like scales, and that term is more familiar and used.

- Because of its reported increased accuracy, interpreters may be overly accepting of reported type and less attentive to verifying type with clients.

- In spite of the wealth of interpretation guidance available, interpreters need experience to acquire comfort and skill in interpreting.

## The MBTI vis-à-vis Other Instruments

There are a number of instruments available that purport to elicit some or all of the personality domains elicited by the MBTI. The instrument most closely comparable to the MBTI is the Jungian Type Survey: The Gray-Wheelright Test (Wheelright, Wheelright, & Buehler, 1964), which was developed by two Jungian analysts, Gray and Wheelright, at about the same time as the MBTI. It has not been widely used outside of Jungian circles. This instrument does not include a J–P scale and has different assumptions about the directionality of the functions, so type dynamics interpretations are somewhat different from those of the MBTI. Nevertheless, this instrument assumes a dynamic interaction of the preferences as does the MBTI.

The two more widely known instruments are the Millon Inventory of Personality Styles (Millon, 1994), which claims to measure Jungian personality type, and the NEO Personality Inventory (Costa & McCrae, 1985), four of whose five scales show clear correlations with the four MBTI dichotomies. This trait-based instrument has therefore been suggested by its authors as an alternative to the MBTI. A detailed critical comparison of the advantages and disadvantages of the MBTI vis-à-vis other instruments is beyond the scope and intent of this chapter. There are several important differences between the MBTI and other instruments that attempt to address the same domains of personality. Awareness of these differences can provide a useful evaluative perspective for people wishing to assess normal personality differences. Differences include the following:

- MBTI dichotomies focus on qualitatively different opposite categories, whereas other instruments explicitly or implicitly ascribe trait meaning to category scores.
- The MBTI is the only major instrument that predicts the specific dynamic interactions among the dichotomies that reflect the Jung/Myers theory, and it reports research evidence in support of these interactions.
- Each pole of each dichotomy is considered to be legitimate and adaptive in its own right; other instruments explicitly or implicitly favor one pole or end of a continuum over the other.
- In the MBTI there is no explicit or implicit definition of one pole of a dichotomy as a deficit in or absence of the opposite pole.

• Definitions of the eight preferences use neutral and positive descriptors; neither pole of a dichotomy is favored over its opposite.

## MAJOR REVIEWS

Six reviews of the MBTI have appeared in the *Mental Measurements Yearbooks*. An additional 44 critiques and critical commentaries were published in various journals and books between 1962 and 1995. All of the *Mental Measurements Yearbook* reviews are included below, as well as several other major critiques of the MBTI. A complete list of reviews, criticisms, and responses relevant to the MBTI can be obtained from the Center for Applications of Psychological Type in Gainesville, Florida (see Rapid Reference 1.5).

### MBTI Review References

Coan, R. W. (1978). Review of the Myers-Briggs Type Indicator. In O. K. Buros (Ed.), *The eighth mental measurements yearbook*. Highland Park, NJ: The Gryphon Press.

Devito, A. J. (1985). Review of the Myers-Briggs Type Indicator. In J. V. Mitchell (Ed.), *The ninth mental measurements yearbook* (pp. 1030–1032). Lincoln: University of Nebraska, Buros Institute of Mental Measurements.

Druckman, D., & Bjork, M. A. (Eds.) (1991). *In the minds' eye: Enhancing human performance*. Washington, DC: National Research Council, National Academy Press.

Mendelsohn, G. A. (1965). Review of the Myers-Briggs Type Indicator. In O. K. Buros (Ed.), *The sixth mental measurements yearbook* (pp. 321–322). Highland Park, NJ: The Gryphon Press.

Pittenger, D. J. (1993). The utility of the Myers-Briggs Type Indicator. *Review of Educational Research, 63*, 467–488.

Siegel, L. (1965). Review of the Myers-Briggs Type Indicator. In O. K. Buros (Ed.), *The sixth mental measurements yearbook* (pp. 325–326). Highland Park, NJ: The Gryphon Press.

Stricker, L. J., & Ross, J. (1962). A description and evaluation of the Myers-Briggs Type Indicator. *Research Bulletin, 6*, 1–180.

Stricker, L. J., & Ross, J. (1964). An assessment of some structural properties of the Jungian personality inventory. *Psychological Reports, 14*, 523–643.

Sundberg, N. D. (1965). Review of the Myers-Briggs Type Indicator. In O. K. Buros (Ed)., *The sixth mental measurements yearbook* (pp. 322–325). Highland Park, NJ: The Gryphon Press.

Wiggins, J. S. (1989). Review of the Myers-Briggs Type Indicator. In J. C. Conoley and J. J. Kramer (Eds.), *The tenth mental measurements yearbook* (pp. 536–538). Lincoln: University of Nebraska, Buros Institute of Mental Measurements.

## 🪶 TEST YOURSELF 🪶

1. **A strength of the MBTI is that it is easy to interpret.** True or False?
2. **Which of the following is *false* regarding the strengths and weaknesses of the MBTI?**
   (a) One strength is the elimination of gender- and age-influenced items.
   (b) Item response theory provides good discrimination around the midpoint of each scale.
   (c) The moderate correlation between the S–N and J–P scales is a problem in need of correction.
   (d) none of the above
3. **Both the template-scorable and self-scorable forms of the MBTI are easier to use than the comparable forms associated with Form G.** True or False?
4. **A weighting method was used to match U.S. census data because the random sample originally collected showed**
   (a) an underrepresentation of all major ethnic groups.
   (b) an overrepresentation of Caucasian females.
   (c) an underrepresentation of African American males.
   (d) both b and c.
5. **The focus in the 1998 manual on type dynamics research rather than correlational research is a major weakness.** True or False?
6. **Why might longtime users of the MBTI resist the methodological and terminology changes introduced with Form M?**
7. **Name one asset and one liability of emphasizing the term *dichotomy* and restricting the term *scale* to psychometric references.**

8. **One listed weakness of the MBTI is the need for experience as a method of becoming excellent in interpreting the MBTI.** True or False?

9. **Which instrument is most similar in assumptions to the MBTI?**

   (a)  the NEO Personality Inventory

   (b)  the Jungian Type Survey

   (c)  the MIPS

   (d)  All these instruments have the same assumptions.

10. **One asset of the MBTI is that neither pole of a dichotomy is favored over its opposite.** True or False?

*Answers:* 1. False; 2. c; 3. True; 4. d; 5. False; 6. People are often reluctant to change from something familiar to something unfamiliar; 7. Asset: "Dichotomy" emphasizes two categories rather than scalar "amounts"; Liability: "Dichotomy" has four syllables and is less familiar to people than "scale"; 8. True; 9. b; 10. True.

Six

# CLINICAL APPLICATIONS OF THE MBTI

The Myers-Briggs Type Indicator personality inventory reveals normal variations in personality. It can therefore provide a context for understanding healthy aspects of the individuality of each client, regardless of the presence of any pathology. From such a vantage point, psychological and emotional problems can be more appropriately assessed, possibly inappropriate diagnoses and perceptions avoided, and treatment styles developed that capitalize on a client's natural proclivities. This way of using the MBTI follows Jung's recommendation that therapists strengthen the patient's conscious approach to establish a solid, safe foundation within which unconscious factors can emerge on their own (Jung, 1954, p. 186). In type terms, this means affirming and strengthening the client's dominant and auxiliary functions *before* dealing with the less conscious tertiary and inferior functions, which are relatively inaccessible to conscious control and direction.

Clinicians can also use the theory of type dynamics and development as a conceptual framework within which to understand and treat clients. You will recall from Chapter 1 that in the Jung/Myers theory, individuals use their dominant function in the preferred attitude of Extraversion or Introversion and their auxiliary function in the corresponding nonpreferred attitude. But suppose someone habitually uses the dominant as well as the auxiliary function in the preferred attitude—for example, an ENFP who extraverts both dominant Intuition *and* auxiliary Feeling, or an INTP who introverts both dominant Thinking and auxiliary Intuition. Or suppose that someone does not have a preference for one pole of a dichotomy over the other—for example, a person who does not have a habitual, reliable way of accessing either Sensing or Intuition. These kinds of problems in type development can be manifested in two ways: Some clients have presenting problems that are a direct function of their difficulty in accessing and expressing their natural type effectively; your understanding of type dynamics can be used therapeutically to help these clients explore and gain confidence in "being themselves." Other clients may have a variety of difficulties unrelated to their type that have nevertheless interfered with or are manifested in their type development; for these clients, focusing on issues of type development may improve their general level of functioning at the same time that it encourages them to persist in working on their other difficulties.

This chapter highlights practical insights that will enable clinicians to take type into account in assessing and treating their clients. The initial focus is on the eight preference poles of the four dichotomies, followed by information about the 16 types. The uses of type in treating couples, families, and in chemical addiction are briefly considered, as well as a perspective on working with type with more seriously disturbed individuals. The chapter concludes with cautions regarding appropriate and inappropriate uses of the MBTI in such areas as learning disabilities, attention-deficit disorder and related behavioral disorders, in general personality assessment, and in assessing the effectiveness of treatment.

Some useful generalizations about both therapists and clients who hold each of the eight preferences have emerged from a combination of empirical research and clinical observations. It can be helpful to keep such information in mind as you interview, assess, and treat clients of different types, recognizing that your own type preferences will serve as a pervasive backdrop to your interactions with clients.

One or another preference can become quickly apparent during an initial interview, or you may recognize a client who is very similar or quite different from you. Tentatively affirming the value of characteristics associated with a hypothesized preference can help a client feel understood and accepted, so rapport is quickly established. With experience, clinicians sometimes find that a new client's whole type seems apparent very early in the therapeutic interaction; there are subtle nuances that are associated with the distinctiveness of one or another type. Of course, it is important to suspend judgment until the usual process of verification has occurred. Nevertheless, tentative understanding of a client's probable type can be helpful, especially in couples therapy when the partners are engaged in "accusing" each other of being different or "doing that just to irritate me."

It is usually therapeutic to share your type with clients, as this can serve as a vehicle for explaining and affirming differences and in dealing with rough spots and misunderstandings that occur during the course of therapy. For example, an Intuitive therapist can explain that it is harder for her to call up specific details of the last session without having those facts in a context. Giving clients information about your own type usually enhances the therapeutic process; however, some clients may incorrectly attribute your comments and suggestions solely to your type, rather than to your expertise, and dismiss them as irrelevant. As with all self-disclosure, discussing your own type with clients must be used selectively, judiciously, and with careful consideration of the client's needs.

## CLINICAL APPLICATIONS OF THE EIGHT PREFERENCES

This section looks at the eight preference poles from the point of view of the therapist's preference in relation to clients who are either opposite or the same in that preference. The focus is on the kind of understanding and misunderstanding that may accompany similarities and differences. The comments below concerning similarities and differences in therapist and client preferences are neither exhaustive nor meant to apply in all cases; rather, they should be taken as suggestive and cautionary examples of some of the typological issues that can emerge.

### Extraversion and Introversion

In a system of opposites, people who are most comfortably themselves while extraverting are likely to be less comfortable introverting, whereas people who are most comfortably themselves introverting, tend to be less comfortable extraverting. For extraverted people, the inner world can be too quiet, too lacking in stimulation, too inactive, too solitary. For introverted people, the outside world can be too loud, too stimulating, too demanding of action, too intrusive. Recent brain-mapping research shows a biological basis for these differences, such that Extraverts' brains appear to be less stimulated than Introverts' brains by the same stimulus (see Myers et al., 1998, for a summary of these and related findings). It appears that Introverts are comfortably stimulated when "inside their heads" and may be overstimulated when interacting with the outside world; Extraverts are comfortably stimulated by the outer environment and understimulated when focusing on the inner world.

Concomitants of Extraversion–Introversion similarities and differences can be readily and frequently observed in the conduct of psychotherapy with individuals, couples, and families. Once a therapist is aware of their impact, however, client preferences can be accommodated rather easily.

### Introverted Therapist and Extraverted Client

Make sure to talk and interact more; what may be a comfortable silence for you may be interpreted by the client as criticism or disapproval. Extraverts tend to think "out loud," so the client may tell you a lot more than you think is necessary to get to the point. Expect Extraverted clients to talk a good deal about what is happening in their lives, their interactions, thoughts, or feeling about others, what they are doing or want to do. Don't assume that they are necessarily avoiding important internal issues; they likely need to let you know who they are in their most comfortable arena before tackling their inner life. They are also likely to see other people and outer events as largely responsible for their problems, and this is natural up to a point. However, continued exclusive focus on the outer world and dismissal of personal contributions to problems may signal a client who has not developed an effective introverted auxiliary function. Such a client may arrange life so as to be continuously active and with other people. Don't assume this is merely due to the client's extraverted preference; such clients may benefit from your encouragement to slowly explore the more unfamiliar and uncomfortable inner side of themselves.

### Introverted Therapist and Client

You will probably be quite accepting of the longer time it takes to establish a comfortable rapport. But be careful not to be overly accepting if your client hesitates to discuss problems; too much "understanding" may validate an Introverted client's fear that his or her thoughts and feelings are abnormal or unacceptable. Acknowledge that self-disclosure is difficult, but encourage the client to risk it. As a fellow Introvert, you may be slow to notice clients who eagerly discuss their inner lives but who talk very little about their functioning in the world. These clients might be having difficulty using and trusting their auxiliary function, which should be their adaptive access to the outer, extraverted world. Try to determine whether the client habitually introverts both dominant and auxiliary, indicating a persistent problem in type development, or whether this is a response to situational factors. If the former, you can help clients gain confidence in extraverting their auxiliary; you can empathize with their fear of failure in this regard but also encourage and support them when they make increasingly frequent forays into the outside world. Clients can also be encouraged to have greater trust in others' positive perceptions and judgments of them. Introverts often devalue themselves. If introverting the auxiliary is transient rather than habitual, you can focus productively on identifying current factors that are pushing a client's normally extraverted function inside.

### Extraverted Therapist and Introverted Client

Talk less and expect less talking from your client. What may be an uncomfortable silence for you is probably necessary reflecting time for the client. In fact, many Introverted clients need a great deal of time to consider a question before being able to answer it. It can be helpful to give such clients homework assignments that encourage them to mull something over and talk about it in the next session. Don't interpret the client's hesitancy to reveal personal information as defensiveness or avoidance; it may take more time than you think necessary to establish a trusting relationship. Try asking fewer questions and making fewer comments, and space everything out over a longer time period; otherwise the client may interpret your natural and genuine enthusiasm, interest, and concern as intrusive and controlling. Don't be too quick to "correct" a client's self-doubt or self-criticism or to recommend a great many extraverted endeavors as a way to overcome any anxiety about being in social situations. Your corrections or recommendations may be taken as yet another confirmation of the client's inadequacy. Introverted clients first look inside themselves as the source of their difficulties, and this is natural. However, after doing that, they should be encouraged to consider the outside world and other people as contributing to problems. A client who talks exclusively about his or her inner life may not have developed an effective extraverted auxiliary function. Be understanding but not overly indulgent of the client's discomfort in extraverting. Validation of a client's attempts to function in the outer world can be helpful, especially coming from an Extraverted therapist.

### Extraverted Therapist and Client

You may very much enjoy seeing the client and may have very comfortable interchanges, since the style of communicating will seem natural and familiar. But it may be harder for you to differentiate between a client whose many activities and relationships are natural and adaptive and one who may be overdoing an outer focus as a way of avoiding being alone and having to face internal issues. Such a client may be one-sidedly extraverting both dominant and auxiliary functions and have little development of inner perception or inner judgment, whichever is the auxiliary function. Depending on your own type development, you may be particularly sensitive to problems that can emerge when clients do not have trust in their inner perception or inner judgment. Such clients are particularly likely to overvalue the perceptions and judgments of other people, since the outside world seems more credible to them than their inner selves. Helping a client become aware of misplaced trust in others is an important way to assist in type development. As a fellow Extravert, you can be naturally understanding of some reluctance to stay very long "inside your head" but can also help the client make brief but increasingly frequent attempts to engage in an inner exploration.

There are a number of important client characteristics that are related to Extraversion and Introversion, regardless of the therapist's preference on this dichotomy.

Extraverted clients

- need the therapist to talk a good deal and give feedback on progress.
- look first to others and external circumstances as the source of their problems.
- may be uncomfortable with too much exploration of their "inner life."
- often recount their activities as a way of communicating who they are.
- sometimes extravert both their dominant and auxiliary functions, making them appear to be "extremely" extraverted. This may be either situational or habitual.

Introverted clients

- need more time to establish a trusting relationship and risk discussing difficult areas.

- need more time to reflect before answering questions.
- look first to themselves as the source of their problems.
- benefit from moderate, gradual encouragement to take extraverted "risks."
- sometimes introvert both their dominant and auxiliary functions, making them appear to be "extremely" introverted; this may be either situational or habitual.

## Sensing and Intuition

When people have opposite preferences on the two perceiving functions, they typically focus their attention and interest on quite different aspects of the world; are naturally attracted to different kinds of information; and place different value on occurrences in the past, the present, and the future. In a therapeutic relationship, client-therapist similarities or differences on this dichotomy can have a major impact on the course of therapy, client and therapist satisfaction, and outcome and termination issues.

### *Therapist Preferring Intuition and Client Preferring Sensing*
Try not to interrupt when the client is giving what seems to you to be an overly detailed account of an event or personal issue. You may think you know where the client is heading, but you could be wrong. Sensing clients want to convey information completely, accurately, and with sufficient detail to ensure that you understand. Interrupting by either finishing the client's sentences or asking possibly extraneous questions may be experienced as your disinterest, failure to listen, or lack of respect for and understanding of the nature of the client's problems. Your Sensing-type client will likely want to confine therapy to the specific issues that motivated his or her seeking help, and may have little interest in other areas that you may believe are worthy of attention. In addition, an intellectual understanding of the problems and the way they are interconnected may not be as important to the client as it is to you. However, don't be surprised when a Sensing-type client seems to be overly impressed by your "trivial" interpretation or pointing out of "obvious" connections between aspects of the client's life. Remember that interrelating disparate behaviors, events, or ideas is not a natural, automatic activity for your client. But once aware of such connections, he or she is likely to make immediate and practical

use of these insights, which can have a lasting impact on the resolution of their problems. When a client with a Sensing preference tells you that things are so much better now and terminates therapy, don't assume that this is "premature" or that he or she is denying or avoiding important issues. It is natural and an appropriate and effective use of therapy for Sensing types to enter therapy for a circumscribed problem, terminate when it is resolved, and perhaps return at a later time for a different specific problem.

### Therapist and Client Preferring Intuition

Both of you may feel "connected" quite quickly and enjoy an easy interchange around issues and alternative solutions. But don't assume that you always know what the client means by the half sentences or rapidly shifting topics that are brought up. Your interpretation of such half-formed or vaguely verbalized statements may be quite different from the client's. There is also likely to be a lot less energy from either of you around collecting specific information. You may find that both you and the client have glossed over important facts and details, such as key personal history information or the day and time of the next appointment. Forcing yourself to review what you know or think you know about the client may be helpful. As a fellow Intuitive, you may also be slow to recognize a client whose one-sided use of Intuition is causing problems in living, for example by neglecting to pay bills or arranging for house maintenance and repairs. Both you and your client may be quite comfortable keeping such problems at a conceptual level. However, you can serve as an effective resource by providing helpful, concrete suggestions from your own possible struggles in this area. You won't be surprised to find that Intuitive clients may welcome an exploration of issues beyond those that motivated seeking help. They will likely want to remain in therapy to deal with them. Be careful to consider whether your mutual attraction to such exploration leaves other practical aspects of the client's life as continuing problems.

### Therapist Preferring Sensing and Client Preferring Intuition

Expect and be tolerant of frequent digressions from whatever topic is being discussed; you can bring the client back to the subject later, and the digression may reveal some important facts and history that you may wish to consider. Bear in mind that Intuitive clients automatically make inferences from whatever you say and that such inferences can be taken and recalled by them as actual facts. Don't be surprised when they insist that you "said something" that you know you didn't say; just clarify your meaning and be aware that such a misunderstanding will likely happen again. You might make a habit of checking out your client's understanding of your comments and suggestions. You can explain that your request is motivated by your different preferences for Sensing and Intuition. Some, but by no means all, Intuitive clients may resist homework assignments and instead prefer an open-ended and exploratory approach in their therapy. You might try reframing any assignments that require attention to specific behaviors. Present them as vehicles to stimulate ideas and generate new information. Homework that requires the use of Sensing perception can be quite valuable for Intuitive clients who are ignoring or minimizing some facts and details in their lives. However, you may reach a point in the therapy where you believe the client's issues have been successfully resolved while the client wants further exploration and more "depth" in the therapy. If the client's desires remain unfulfilled, he or she may acknowledge that you helped but feel dissatisfied with the overall outcome of therapy.

### *Therapist and Client Preferring Sensing*
Both of you are likely to be comfortable in following prescribed treatment methods, and you will be quite appreciative of the client's attempts at accuracy and completeness. You probably won't have too many gaps in the information you collect. Sticking to a circumscribed presenting problem may feel appropriate for both of you, as will practical, behavior-focused exercises and detailed homework assignments. However, many Sensing-type clients have difficulty coming up with alternative perspectives and possibilities in relation to their presenting problems—especially in imagining any positive outcomes. These clients will very much benefit from and trust your suggestions in this regard. Your Sensing-type client is likely to appreciate your down-to-earth, practical approach to what may seem to be overwhelming and insoluble problems. As a fellow Sensing type, you may be vulnerable to agreeing with such a client's perspective. Be careful not to "buy into" the client's fears that nothing will ever change for the better. You can point out that since the future is not predictable, staying focused on what can be done now is more worthy of attention.

There are a number of important client characteristics that are related to Sensing and Intuition, regardless of the therapist's preference on this dichotomy. Sensing clients

- want to be accurate, detailed, and complete in their communications.
- benefit from being provided with alternative explanations and possible outcomes.
- use therapy productively to deal with specific, circumscribed problems.
- are relatively uninterested in broad-ranging explorations of their psyches.
- can be so one-sidedly devoted to Sensing as to appear rigidly present-oriented and fact focused, rejecting all alternative perspectives.
- gain practical insights from therapist interpretations and use new perspectives to help resolve their problems.

Intuitive clients

- frequently digress from the subject being discussed and want to go where their Intuition leads them.
- make inferences from therapist statements, which may be incorrect or distorted.
- may be unenthusiastic about specific, behavioral homework assignments.
- are often intrigued by an exploration of their psyche and wish to remain in therapy longer.
- may be one-sided in their use of Intuition, flitting from one idea and possibility to another, while avoiding facts and details that later create serious life problems.
- may remain "stuck" when the insights they gain are not actualized in concrete behavior.

## Thinking and Feeling

Differences and similarities in the way client and therapist arrive at conclusions can lead to troublesome misunderstandings and unconscious projections and counterprojections during the therapeutic process. The

Thinking–Feeling dichotomy brings forth issues of acceptance, understanding, empathy, objectivity, language and communication style, and myriad other factors relevant to the conduct of therapy. It is therefore especially important for therapists to understand these very different approaches to judgment so that they can avoid communicating unintended judgments to their clients—both those who have opposite preferences in judgment and those who share their preference.

### Therapist Preferring Feeling and Client Preferring Thinking

Don't expect your client to talk easily or directly about his or her emotions and deeply held values, and don't mistake the infrequent use of "feeling" words to reflect an absence of strong emotions. People who prefer Thinking tend to have fewer words to describe what they are feeling than do Feeling types, since they habitually make judgments by excluding their own and others' emotions and values from the decision-making process. This makes them relatively inexperienced in describing the feeling or valuing realm, so it is harder for them to come up with words that reflect the nuances of Feeling evaluation. Asking the client what he or she *thinks,* rather than *feels,* is a simple but effective way to elicit the desired information. Insistence on a feeling focus or emotional response will likely cause the client considerable distress and diminish your credibility as a therapist. Often, but not always, Thinking-type clients have readier access to anger than to other emotions; be aware that such anger may often be a global response to hurt, disappointment, frustration, or a variety of other emotions that the client may not be able to conceptualize and verbalize. Exploring this possibility could prove fruitful, especially when framed within a cognitive or systems approach to therapy, which is likely to be an approach that is appealing to your Thinking-type client. It is natural for people who prefer Thinking to be concerned about your competence and credentials; try not to take their questions as criticisms or challenges. Nondefensively stating your training, experience, and credentials can establish your credibility and be the basis for trust in your expertise. Bear in mind that for some Thinking types, seeking help from a mental health professional may be experienced as an especially distressing personal failure. It is advisable not to express your natural empathy and understanding too enthusiastically, as your client may see this as patronizing and this may diminish your credibility as a therapist. Your Thinking-type client may not put as much importance on the therapeutic relationship as you do, and you may need to keep therapy at an "intellectual" level for much longer than you would like. Both the nature of the therapeutic relationship and enabling the client to express emotions will likely be more important to you than to the client. But don't ignore the emotional area forever; eventually it will be safe for the client to risk emotional expression. Bear in mind, however, that this can be quite uncomfortable for a Thinking type, who well may fear that once unleashed, emotions will be uncontrollable.

### Therapist and Client Preferring Feeling

You will likely become comfortable with each other quickly and your easy understanding and use of Feeling language will encourage rapport and a sense of trust. You can capitalize on your similar judging approach to help a client whose use of Feeling is one-sided and exaggerated to consider the logical consequences of decisions. Such clients often "stop" at the experience of negative feeling so they have no opportunity to look at either the long-term logical or value consequences of their decisions. Discussing a worst-case scenario is an effective technique to help clients move beyond this point. It often becomes apparent to such a client that they can indeed tolerate the immediate pain of a confrontation or negatively charged event to avoid a far more significant pain at a later time. Ask whether the client can recall ever having avoided telling the truth or having "told a white lie" to spare someone else pain or hurt, only to have this come back to haunt him or her by ultimately creating an even worse situation. Confronting such events in their lives can help Feeling-type clients develop better Feeling judgments and thereby avoid making purely "emotional" decisions. As a Feeling-type therapist, you can also help Feeling-type clients to better interpret the language used by the Thinking types in their lives; you can point out that it is to be expected that people whose nature is to discover flaws, errors, and inconsistencies will first focus on what is wrong; mentioning what is correct and working well seems to Thinking types to be unnecessary and patronizing.

### Therapist Preferring Thinking and Client Preferring Feeling

Your client can interpret your dispassionate approach as a lack of concern and empathy, and feel that he or she is not someone worthy of your attention. Such a client may take your comments and observations as disapproval and criticism. It can be helpful to qualify what you say, making sure to include modifiers like "may" or "seems to." Don't assume that your Feeling-type client will openly disagree with you or tell you how they feel about you; many Feeling types are uncomfortable doing this and see questioning others' statements and judgments as contentious. It is therefore helpful to give them "permission" to disagree by saying things like, "I could be mistaken, but" or "One way of seeing this is . . ." You may be more oriented to cognitive, behavioral, and systems approaches, whereas your Feeling clients may expect more affective, client-focused methods. Try to accommodate your client while not abandoning what works for you. The client may benefit from your particular approach, as long as it is undertaken in a context of care, empathy, and attentiveness. Bear in mind, however, that it is natural for Feeling types to want verbal confirmation of your continuing interest and concern; don't assume that when they seek this from you they are being overly needy and lacking a sense of self.

### Therapist and Client Preferring Thinking

You will likely find it easy to connect with each other, and your client may find your approach to therapy appealing and comfortable. Thinking-type clients are far less likely to interpret your declarative statements as lack of understanding and may be relieved when you don't insist on early emotional disclosures. However, you both may risk ignoring what is important and meaningful to the client and talk around rather than about relationship issues, possible fears about losing control of one's emotions, and deeply held values. The client may not be able to articulate such issues. Judicious self-disclosure by you in this area may encourage the client to risk the awkwardness of attempting to communicate about this usually nonarticulated area.

There are a number of important client characteristics that are related to Thinking and Feeling, regardless of the therapist's preference on this dichotomy.

Thinking-type clients

- have fewer words to describe feeling values and emotions than Feeling-type clients do.
- may tell you what they feel when asked what they "think."
- sometimes display a variety of emotions by expressing anger.

- will be concerned about the therapist's competence and credentials.
- may fear that once expressed, their emotions will be uncontrollable.
- if one-sidedly devoted to Thinking, can avoid and deny that feeling and emotion play any part in their lives.

Feeling-type clients

- may interpret a dispassionate therapeutic approach as distant and uncaring.
- can take casual comments and observations as criticisms.
- are often reluctant to disagree with the therapist's statements.
- prefer affective, client-centered therapeutic approaches.
- naturally need verbal affirmation of the therapist's interest and concern.
- if one-sidedly devoted to Feeling, can avoid any kind of confrontation or unpleasantness.

## Judging and Perceiving

The observable behavior of both clients and therapists is often related to the preference for a Judging or a Perceiving approach to the outer world. Therapists and clients can draw either positive or negative conclusions from each others' way of dealing with schedules, deadlines, new information, and the desire for or discomfort with plans and conclusions. Client and therapist similarities and differences on this dichotomy often relate to how therapy is structured and the predictability of the process. Therapists can use their understanding of differences in the J and P preference to avoid inappropriate inferences about the client and to "explain" people with the opposite preference to their clients.

### Therapist Preferring Perceiving and Client Preferring Judging

Your client is unlikely to feel comfortable with an open-ended, exploratory style and will want goals, time lines, and expected outcomes to be issues for joint exploration. Dismissing legitimate concerns in this area can diminish the client's trust and respect for you and your expertise. You may need to resist inquiring immediately about ancillary areas that come up during a discussion because to do so may be disruptive to a client who wants to finish one topic before moving on to another. And if you both agreed to cover something in the next session, it's a good idea to stick to the plan. It is even more important to be aware that statements that you intend as possibilities rather than firm conclusions or decisions may be taken by your client as final plans. What is a comfortable "loose end" that you'll decide about later may be a clear judgment in your client's mind. It is natural for clients with a Judging preference to obsess about small matters, especially when experiencing moderate stress. Don't mistake this for a psychological disorder. What is often helpful for a Judging client in this state is to be able to obsess out loud without fear of having concerns minimized or of being given advice.

### Therapist and Client Preferring Perceiving
You will both likely be comfortable with an open-ended and free-ranging approach to issues, moving easily within and between topics. But you may find that you end up without the information you were seeking because you were both led astray. Chances are the missed topic will resurface eventually, and you may both accept this as natural. But be alert to the possibility that the client's natural proclivities in this regard may sometimes reflect "changing the subject" because it is an uncomfortable one. This may become apparent when you bring the discussion back to an earlier topic. Your shared preference for delaying decision making may lead you to be slow to recognize actual self-destructive procrastinating by the client, and you may be overly sympathetic to his or her expression of helplessness regarding "getting organized" or meeting deadlines. Such clients may be responding to internal or external stress by exaggerating their natural affinity for gathering information (Perceiving preference) to the point that they are perpetually distracted. It is important to determine whether such a response is habitual or situational and treat both possiblities as issues to be addressed in therapy.

### Therapist Preferring Judging and Client Preferring Perceiving
Try to be tolerant of some amount of drifting off topic on the client's part or of the client's wanting to further discuss an area that you thought had been brought to closure. Try to delay coming to any conclusions about what is going on with this client, since he or she is likely to add important information, possibly outside of its original context. Be aware that some Perceiving clients can be rather lax about schedules and appointment times. Don't assume they

are being "resistant" or oppositional, but don't be too accepting of it either; the behavior in therapy may well reflect similar issues that have broad and pervasive consequences in the client's relationships and at work. Perceiving clients may expect you to be directive and to tell them what to attend to in their lives, especially if stress and conflicting demands have pushed their natural information-gathering approach to the level of distractibility. Such clients can benefit from your help in limiting their focus to the essentials. Guidance in prioritizing can eventually lead them to take control by themselves and use their introverted Judging function to select among the many options available through their preferred Perceiving function.

### Therapist and Client Preferring Judging

Both you and your client may function well using a systems model of therapy rather than process or structural models. However, your client's whole type will influence whether and which therapy approach will prove most effective in individual treatment. Therapeutic goals, schedules, and time frames will be comfortable for you both, but be careful that in your desire to achieve closure, you don't reach conclusions prematurely and shut off further data collection. Your client may not pick up on such an oversight, being of the same attitude; it may well be worthwhile to revisit issues that had appeared to both of you to be resolved. You are in a good position to understand and help a client who obsesses about details when experiencing stress. Referring to your own Judging preference and disclosing that you too obsess in the same way can be quite affirming to a client who fears that his behavior may be out of bounds or pathological.

There are a number of important client characteristics that are related to Judging and Perceiving, regardless of the therapist's preference on this dichotomy.

Judging clients

- appreciate plans, schedules, and defined therapeutic goals.
- may interpret tentative suggestions or possibilities as firm intentions and decisions.
- tend to obsess about small things, especially when experiencing stress.
- often prefer systems approaches to psychotherapy.
- may reach closure on an issue prematurely.

• benefit from being encouraged to reconsider their judgments and look at other options.

Perceiving clients

• appreciate a casual, open-ended approach to therapy and therapeutic goals.
• may move from one topic to another with no need for closure of any one issue.
• may see the therapist's stated intention or conclusion as one of many possibilities still open for consideration.
• can become aimless and distracted, especially when experiencing stress.
• may want the therapist to be directive and tell them what to do.
• benefit from help with prioritizing and choosing among the many options they perceive.

## THE 16 TYPES

The 16 types are not equally attracted to counseling and psychotherapy, either as therapists or as clients. For therapists, there are type-related differences in theoretical orientations and preferred treatment modalities; for clients, there is wide variation in presenting issues, expectations, and therapeutic goals. As is the case when considering single preferences, conjunctions of therapist and client type can present potential pitfalls and likely assets. The focus in this section is on client characteristics that are associated with whole type. Information about therapists of each type is also summarized.

Readers should be cautious in generalizing from the summaries below, since there are wide within-type differences as well as variations in type development of clients. Useful compilations of material relevant to assessment and psychotherapy are included in the annotated bibliography that concludes this book. The information here and in various publications can help orient your exploration of type in your own work with clients. It can be helpful to conceive of type as a basic template on which a broad range of client issues can be overlaid.

The two types who share the same dominant function are discussed together and similarities and differences are highlighted. Observations about clients of these types appear first, followed by points about therapists of each dominant type. The types are presented in the same order as in *Introduction to Type* (Myers, 1998). As a reminder, the dynamics of each type are shown first.

## Dominant Introverted Sensing Types

|  | *ISTJ* | *ISFJ* |
|---|---|---|
| Dominant | Introverted Sensing | Introverted Sensing |
| Auxiliary | Extraverted Thinking | Extraverted Feeling |
| Tertiary | Feeling | Thinking |
| Inferior | Extraverted Intuition | Extraverted Intuition |

### *ISTJ and ISFJ Clients*

ISFJs are more likely than ISTJs to see a counselor or therapist for personal problems, though both types may be referred by a physician for stress-related somatic symptoms. Both types seek expert advice for academic, career, or rehabilitation issues. Introverted Sensing types, who value stability, loyalty, and social traditions seem to be particularly vulnerable to stressors such as rapid environmental and social change and uncertainties in the workplace. Knowing that their reactions are natural expressions of their type can be affirming to clients and useful in developing helpful interventions. In addition, therapists should be aware of the following characteristics of Introverted Sensing clients.

ISTJ clients

- sometimes seek therapy for a personal problem as a result of successful couples therapy—usually with the same therapist.
- favor short-term, focused techniques and terminate as soon as the problem is resolved.
- often present a calm, controlled exterior, while experiencing great inner turmoil and fear of losing control.
- under stress, are pessimistic about the future and imagine negative possibilities, which therapists may see as resistance to treatment.
- may be judged as obsessive-compulsive when they are actually demonstrating their natural desire for organization, order, and predictability.

- more readily become engaged in the treatment proess when the therapist communicates that he or she understands their perspective.
- if both dominant Sensing and auxiliary Thinking are habitually introverted, will appear rigid, inaccessible, out of contact with their own and other's emotions, and resistant to change.

ISFJ clients

- May self-refer or be referred for anxiety, depression, and stress-related somatic symptoms.
- like supportive, cognitive approaches and are conscientious about homework assignments.
- readily show that they are in distress, despairing, and feeling unable to cope.
- under stress, see only negative outcomes in the future but are likely to comply with therapist suggestions when given sufficient understanding and encouragement.
- may be judged as codependent, when they are actually demonstrating the caring, helpfulness, and responsibility that is fulfilling for their type.
- benefit from being helped to see psychological connections and alternative explanations of their own and others' behavior.
- if both dominant Sensing and auxiliary Feeling are introverted, can appear inflexible, unwilling or unable to communicate their needs and desires, passively critical, and rigidly moralistic.

### ISTJ or ISFJ Therapists
There are some natural areas of comfort, discomfort, and bias that may emerge when working with clients of different types, especially those who prefer Intuition. You should not assume that a practical, focused approach is inappropriate for these clients, as it can be effective for very different reasons than would be true for you. However, clients who are oriented to long-term, insight-oriented therapy may choose to work further with someone else after their presenting issues have been resolved. The characteristics of Introverted Sensing therapists that are summarized below should not be taken as hard and fast rules, since therapists of the same type can be quite varied in the approaches that appeal to them.

ISTJ therapists

- are infrequent in comparison to other types.
- favor short-term cognitive/behavioral methods over long-term, affect-oriented, client-centered, or psychodynamic methods.
- like a practical, goal-directed approach to client problems and assign focused homework and specific exercises.
- are more often attracted to career counseling, chemical dependency treatment, and academic counseling than to personal counseling.
- may see their opposite type, ENFPs, as immature, histrionic, irresponsible, and poorly adapted, projecting their own inferior Intuition and tertiary Feeling onto the client.

ISFJ therapists

- enjoy doing counseling that encourages a supportive personal relationship with clients, such as occupational, career, and rehabilitation counseling.
- take a practical, goal-directed, and empathetic approach to client problems and assign homework and exercises specific to those problems.
- are more attracted to short-term, focused, cognitive and behavioral treatment methods than to psychodynamic methods.
- place value on the therapeutic relationship but may be reluctant to confront sensitive issues with clients.
- may see their opposites, ENTPs, as manipulative, uncooperative, and antagonistic.

## Dominant Extraverted Sensing Types

|  | *ESTP* | *ESFP* |
| --- | --- | --- |
| Dominant | Extraverted Sensing | Extraverted Sensing |
| Auxiliary | Introverted Thinking | Introverted Feeling |
| Tertiary | Feeling | Thinking |
| Inferior | Introverted Intuition | Introverted Intuition |

### ESTP and ESFP Clients

ESFPs are more likely to seek professional help than ESTPs, but both types prefer short-term, focused approaches. Their natural affinity for action in the outside world discourages excessive reflection and exploration of inner complexities. A therapist who suggests a relatively simple shift in perspective can help such a client resolve what seemed to be an unsolvable problem. Both types are likely to terminate therapy when they feel better and are unlikely to be interested in intense psychological exploration for its own sake. In addition, therapists should be aware of the following characteristics of Extraverted Sensing clients.

ESTP clients

- may seek help (especially females) when unable to shake depression associated with a failed relationship; males are more likely to talk to a trusted friend rather than a therapist.
- like very short-term, focused approaches and terminate when they feel better and reconnect with their typical sense of competence.
- enjoy discussing their own and others' behavior but are unlikely to imagine hidden motives and complicated interconnections.
- under stress may lose their objectivity and attention to others' needs, misreading others' motives and ascribing meaning to unconnected events.
- may be judged as shallow and self-centered when they demonstrate their natural focus on experiencing the world and the present moment completely and intensely.
- benefit from having realistic options pointed out, since they often have difficulty thinking of options on their own.
- if both dominant Sensing and auxiliary Thinking are extraverted, can appear selfish, fickle, and uncaring of others' needs.

ESFP clients

- may seek help for depression and difficulty coping with both work and personal stress.
- like short-term, supportive approaches that offer practical solutions, and the freedom to come in for sessions on an as-needed basis.
- may reveal anxiety about being seen as immature by family, friends, and the therapist.
- under stress feel confused and overwhelmed by inner associations and possibilities, easily misinterpreting others' motives and behavior.
- may be judged as shallow, self-centered, and overly concerned with

appearances and material possessions, in their natural focus on esthetic and sensual aspects of life.

• benefit from frequent reassurance that the future will not be an inevitable continuation of the present, and from help with priorities and contingency plans.

• if both dominant Sensing and auxiliary Feeling are extraverted, will be anxious about and overvalue others' judgments and have little sense of their own worth.

## ESTP or ESFP Therapists

Short-term, focused approaches rather than long-term exploratory therapy will likely make the most sense to you. Clients who are interested in the interconnections and complexities of their inner life will likely be dissatisfied with your pragmatic approach, but they will appreciate your help in times of crisis. In fact, you may be attracted to crisis work, mediation, focused group therapy, and the practical implementation of treatment programs. ESFPs may enjoy working with children as well. The characteristics of Extraverted Sensing therapists that are summarized below should not be taken as hard and fast rules, since therapists of the same type can be quite varied in the approaches that appeal to them.

ESTP therapists

• are infrequent in comparison to other types.

• are attracted to crisis counseling and may enjoy working with acting-out adolescents and adults with behavioral problems, where their to-the-point, no-nonsense approach can be very effective.

• can capitalize on their focused, pragmatic approach to calm down highly stressed or disturbed clients of all types.

• may be impatient with or disparaging of psychodynamic, "intuitive" therapy styles, seeing them as unfocused and unnecessarily complex.

• may see their opposite, INFJs, as vague, fragile, with "loose associations," or even delusional and paranoid.

ESFP therapists

• are infrequent in comparison to other types.

• are likely to enjoy working directly with young children, adolescents, and adults who respond positively to an optimistic, yet realistic, approach to their problems.

- are seen by clients as trustworthy and genuinely interested in their welfare.
- easily create a positive atmosphere and genuine optimism about client problems.
- may see INTJs and INFJs as overly serious, intense, and out of touch with reality.

## Dominant Introverted Intuitives

|  | *INTJ* | *INFJ* |
|---|---|---|
| Dominant | Introverted Intuition | Introverted Intuition |
| Auxiliary | Extraverted Thinking | Extraverted Feeling |
| Tertiary | Feeling | Thinking |
| Inferior | Extraverted Sensing | Extraverted Sensing |

### *INTJ and INFJ Clients*

These clients may seek therapy because of dissatisfactions with personal and work relationships, a vague sense of alienation from the world, and a desire to understand their lives in depth. Validating their sense of being different by pointing out their infrequency in the general population (INFJ males and INTJ females are least frequent) can be helpful, as can an understanding of the ways their typological makeup is consistent with their search for meaning and feelings of estrangement. They want to focus on intrapsychic connections and human complexity, both their own and that of others. In addition, therapists should be aware of the following characteristics of Introverted Intuitive clients.

INTJ clients

- may seek therapy for in-depth understanding and persistent feelings of alienation from others.
- like long-term, psychodynamic approaches as well as cognitive and systems approaches.
- come across as serious, intense, and complex and may not easily express emotions.

- under stress become intensely focused on minor details in the outside world and may overdo sensual activities such as eating, drinking, and exercising.
- may be judged as obsessive or out of touch with reality, in their natural affinity for organizing disparate and complex data in innovative ways.
- benefit from examining themselves at a conceptual level and are unlikely to accept interpretations and suggestions without questioning their rationale.
- if both dominant Intuition and auxiliary Thinking are introverted, may lack confidence and be unaware of their abilities, feeling estranged from others and unable to relate.

INFJ clients

- may seek therapy for depression, self-doubt, or a quest for inner growth and development.
- like spiritual and philosophical approaches and find cognitive-behaviorial methods unappealing.
- are likely to acknowledge a fear of "being crazy," due to their uncanny awareness of others' thoughts and feelings, which others may not recognize until much later.
- under stress may dwell obsessively on outer events, remarks, slights, and perceived injustices, as well as engaging in excessive sensual activities as do INTJs.
- can find it extremely helpful when the therapist explains the typological basis of their "uncanny" awareness, as well as providing them with reassurance about their mental stability.
- if both dominant Intuition and auxiliary Feeling are introverted, may appear as ill equipped to function in the world and may read unintended meaning into people's comments, including those of the therapist.

### INTJ and INFJ Therapists

You probably have an impressive ability to organize, integrate, and make sense of very complex and broad-ranging client difficulties. Introverted Intuitive therapists can quickly zero in on a client's central concern, even when the client is only dimly aware that it is a core issue. If you are an INTJ, try to qualify your statements and observations with modifiers such as "may," "seems to," "one way of seeing this," and so on. Otherwise, clients may believe you are giving them dicta that are not open to disagreement. If you are an INFJ, your uncanny ability to intuit your client's thoughts and feelings may awe some clients, who may believe you can read their minds. Your empathetic guidance can be especially helpful to types who are overwhelmed by the disorganization in their lives, often the dominant Extraverted Intuitive types. The characteristics of Introverted Intuitive therapists that are summarized below should not be taken as hard and fast rules, since therapists of the same type can be quite varied in the approaches that appeal to them.

INTJ therapists

- are likely to be comfortable using a psychodynamic or systems approach to therapy.
- especially enjoy clients who are interested in exploring psychological complexities.
- may appear to have "uncanny" understanding of client's thoughts and feelings.
- can be perceived by clients, especially Feeling types, as critical and judgmental.
- may have difficulty accepting the practical, present orientation of ESFP and ESTP clients, seeing them as shallow, self-centered, and unable to deal with complexity.

INFJ therapists

- are frequently attracted to counseling and psychotherapy as a career.
- like insight-oriented, psychodynamic, and cognitive approaches that facilitate client growth and development.
- are seen by clients as insightful, committed, caring, and empathetic.
- may sometimes disregard a client's problems in everyday living while focusing on broader issues of development.
- may see practical, Sensing-type clients as resistant or unmotivated, and particularly dislike working with clients who withhold or distort information about themselves.

## Dominant Extraverted Intuitives

|  | *ENTP* | *ENFP* |
|---|---|---|
| Dominant | Extraverted Intuition | Extraverted Intuition |
| Auxiliary | Introverted Thinking | Introverted Feeling |
| Tertiary | Feeling | Thinking |
| Inferior | Introverted Sensing | Introverted Sensing |

### ENTP and ENFP Clients

ENFPs are far more likely to seek psychological help than ENTPs; however, people of both types may enter therapy for problems and dissatisfactions with relationships and depression arising from this. ENTPs and ENFPs often thrive in fast-paced, rapidly changing environments and seem well able to handle situations that other types may experience as stressful. ENFPs are typically much more comfortable as psychotherapy clients than ENTPs. In addition, therapists should be aware of the following characteristics of Extraverted Intuitive clients.

ENTP clients

- may want help with unfamiliar internal distress and self-doubt.
- are likely to accept any therapeutic approach that does not seem intellectually simplistic.
- may initially need to demonstrate their competence and cleverness and therefore challenge the therapist's competence.
- under stress may be likely to increase their high activity level, "crash," and become uncharacteristically ruminative and focused on internal details and body symptoms.
- may be judged as manipulative, insensitive, and arrogant in their natural enjoyment of lively arguments and their focus on intellectual virtuosity.
- are likely to benefit from having their competence and worthiness unobtrusively accepted by the therapist as a necessary step in establishing trust and a willingness to disclose doubts and fears.
- if both dominant Intuition and auxiliary Thinking are habitually extraverted, may be especially prone to distressing midlife reactions, sometimes becoming involved in "inappropriate" romantic relationships.

ENFP clients

- seek help for specific personal and relationship problems as well as for guidance related to their intense interest in growth and development.
- will accept any approach that recognizes their individuality and permits freedom to go off on tangents and explore psychological complexities.
- can appear histrionic and ungrounded, often reporting a history of being seen by others as flightly, irresponsible, and unfocused.
- may not recognize when their high stress tolerance has surpassed its typical level and then become depressed, obsessed with small details, and focused on bodily symptoms.
- may be judged as overly emotional, irresponsible, and unrealistic in their natural exuberance and focus on experiencing stimulating and emotionally meaningful relationships and projects.
- may benefit from the therapist's help in organizing at least some of life's details and guidance in choosing which projects to pursue.
- if both dominant Intuition and auxiliary Feeling are habitually extraverted, may legitimately doubt their inner substance and be quite vulnerable to others' positive and negative projections.

### ENTP or ENFP Therapists

You probably like therapeutic approaches that rely on ingenuity in making connections among ideas and events. ENFPs are more likely to enjoy client-centered, affective approaches, whereas ENTPs prefer cognitive and systems methods. Active engagement with clients is appealing to both types. Your natural ability to attend to many interactions at the same time can be particularly useful in family and group therapy. Some Introverted clients may feel overpowered by your Extraversion, so you need to be especially careful to avoid conveying that you are critical of or impatient with a client's progress or willingness to take risks. The characteristics of Extraverted Intuitive therapists that are summarized below should not be taken as hard and fast rules, since therapists of the same type can be quite varied in the approaches that appeal to them.

ENTP therapists

- are attracted to cognitive approaches, like other Thinking types.
- are one of two Thinking types that are not significantly overrepresented among behavioral psychologists.

- may be impatient or uninterested in clients who want to focus on feelings and internal growth rather than directly resolving problems in the outside world.
- are likely to be confrontive with clients, which some Feeling types may experience as intimidating.
- may judge ISFJ and ISTJ clients as maladaptive in their conscientious, orderly approach to life.

ENFP therapists

- are overrepresented as counselors and psychotherapists.
- focus on the client's potential for growth, regardless of the severity of their symptoms.
- are comfortable in taking a nurturing, encouraging role with clients.
- risk evaluating clients of very different types as unmotivated, uncooperative, and pessimistic.
- can readily see ISTJ and INTJ clients as negative, rigid, and compulsive.

## Introverted Thinking Types

|           | *ISTP*               | *INTP*               |
|-----------|----------------------|----------------------|
| Dominant  | Introverted Thinking | Introverted Thinking |
| Auxiliary | Extraverted Sensing  | Extraverted Intuition |
| Tertiary  | Intuition            | Sensing              |
| Inferior  | Extraverted Feeling  | Extraverted Feeling  |

### *ISTP and INTP Clients*

Both Introverted Thinking types prefer solving their own problems through the detached application of logic. ISTPs are usually referred by someone else; INTPs may seek help on their own when they are unable to understand what they experience as irrational thoughts and emotions. Both types can appear calm and detached when they are actually feeling confused and afraid of losing control of their emotions. They may also report difficulty in personal and work relationships because of their insistence on maintaining independence of action and their strong desire to be in control of how they use their time. Therapists should also be aware of the following characteristics of Introverted Thinking clients.

ISTP clients

- are not very likely to seek therapy but may be referred for stress-related somatic symptoms or reluctantly participate in couples therapy.
- favor short-term, focused approaches and are likely to respond to queries briefly and with few digressions.
- may present a distant, critical, and uncaring demeanor, which may mask intense devotion, warmth, and caring for a few intimate others.
- under stress can become even more abrupt and critical than usual and then express uncharacteristic feelings of emotional hurt and a conviction that they are unloved.
- may be judged as oppositional and resistant in their natural focus on the reality of facts that lead to inevitable logical conclusions.
- benefit from guidance in considering alternative points of view and outcomes and in becoming aware of how others interpret their words and actions.
- if both dominant Thinking and auxiliary Sensing are habitually introverted, can appear hypercritical, abrupt to the point of rudeness, and lacking in compassion.

INTP clients

- are more likely than ISTPs to seek help with personal problems but may initially put therapy within a framework of intellectual curiosity.
- are likely to be more concerned with the competence of the therapist than the particular approach used.
- may need to keep therapy at a conceptual level for a long time before risking emergence of painful emotions.
- under stress become hypersensitive to signs they are disliked or excluded and can become uncharacteristically emotional.
- benefit from help in understanding others' motives and behaviors and in reassurance that once lost, emotional control will be regained.
- if both dominant Thinking and auxiliary Intuition are habitually introverted, can be out of touch with the demands of the outer world and devote all their energy to the pursuit of a single interest.

### ISTP or INTP Therapists

You will find few members of your type in the field if you are an ISTP, and many more as an INTP. Both of your types are likely to be comfortable with cognitive approaches and INTPs in particular will see the complexities of client behavior as an interesting challenge. ISTPs bring their directness and pragmatism to the task; INTPs can offer conceptual clarity and a calm, dispassionate approach. Both may be seen by some Feeling-type clients as somewhat distant and critical. The characteristics of Introverted Thinking therapists that are summarized below should not be taken as hard and fast rules, since therapists of the same type can be quite varied in the approaches that appeal to them.

ISTP therapists

- are infrequent in comparison to other types.
- have a pragmatic perspective, which is useful in mediation situations.
- care deeply about clients and may demonstrate this by actions rather than words.
- may be impatient with clients and colleagues who favor psychodynamic approaches.
- may see their opposite types, ENFJs and ESFJs, as excessively emotional and physically and psychologically intrusive.

INTP therapists

- are more frequent than ISTP therapists.
- enjoy both cognitive and psychodynamic approaches to therapy.
- are unlikely to use Affective approaches to therapy.
- need to be alert to client's feelings of therapist disapproval or disinterest.
- may see their opposite types, ESFJs and ENFJs, as in much more emotional distress than these clients actually feel and may be uncomfortable working with them.

## Dominant Extraverted Thinking Types

|  | *ESTJ* | *ENTJ* |
| --- | --- | --- |
| Dominant | Extraverted Thinking | Extraverted Thinking |
| Auxiliary | Introverted Sensing | Introverted Intuition |
| Tertiary | Intuition | Sensing |
| Inferior | Introverted Feeling | Introverted Feeling |

### ESTJ and ENTJ Clients

These typically high-energy, self-confident people may seek help when a chronic illness emerges that demands a lifestyle change or when a very important relationship is threatened or ends. They are naturally achievement oriented and competitive and enjoy the challenge of directing others to produce an effective outcome. Situations that force them to recognize the "irrationality" of their own and others' emotions can be quite upsetting to them. Such situations often occur in the context of intimate relationships. Extraverted Thinking types may view therapy as a last resort and correspondingly interpret their need for help as a defeat and failure. They are by nature challenging and critical, and are likely to take this same approach with regard to a therapist's skills and approach. Therapists should also be aware of the following characteristics of Extraverted Thinking clients.

ESTJ clients

- do not often seek psychotherapy but may come for help with extreme emotional reactions or as part of a couple. They may also be referred for help with required lifestyle changes.
- prefer short-term, problem-solving approaches that focus directly on the issues; may try to direct the therapeutic process.
- can be experiencing quite a bit of inner distress and self-doubt while maintaining a competent, controlled demeanor.
- under stress fear they will (and often do) lose control and are subject to emotional outbursts, feeling others to be uncaring and unappreciative.
- may be judged as motivated solely by a need to control and dominate others, when they are exercising their natural desire to organize the world and produce results.
- can experience relief and affirmation from an explanation of why they feel vulnerable and emotionally out of control.
- if both dominant Thinking and auxiliary Sensing are habitually extraverted, may come across as rigidly overly controlling, impatient, and hypercritical.

ENTJ clients

- may seek therapy for relationship problems or help recovering from perceived personal failures.
- like an approach that provides structure and focuses on getting desired results.

- can try to direct the therapy and the therapist, since asking for help with personal problems is unfamiliar and unacceptable.
- under stress may be flooded with uncontrollable emotion and fear they will never regain control.
- may be judged as power hungry and arrogantly self-confident, when exercising their natural interest in competent management, long-range planning, and implementation of their clear vision of future outcomes.
- will respond positively when the therapist acknowledges their discomfort in the client role but firmly asserts her or his expertise and intent to direct the therapy.
- if both dominant Thinking and auxiliary Intuition are habitually extraverted, can appear arrogantly domineering and dismissive of other's needs and ideas.

## ESTJ or ENTJ Therapists

You may be attracted to the field because of the opportunities it provides to satisfy your interest in people as well as your fascination with the ways people behave and interact in organizational contexts. If you are an ESTJ, you may enjoy working with individual clients in an organization to achieve specific goals, as well as in career applications; if you are an ENTJ, you may get satisfaction from applying psychological principles to broad organizational goals. Both ESTJs and ENTJs tend to like working with groups of people, as in structured and focused team building or group therapy.

ESTJ therapists

- are infrequent in comparison to other types, and as therapists, find behavioral approaches compatible with their outlook.
- are likely to prefer organizational consulting and career counseling that focuses on practical problem resolution.
- favor structured, systematic approaches and like working with clear procedures and defined goals.
- may be seen by some clients, Feeling–Perceiving types for example, as competent, but critical and directive.
- may see their opposite types, INFP, as timid, fragile, overly sensitive, and uncommunicative.

ENTJ therapists

- are more attracted to the field than their ESTJ companion type.
- favor behavioral, cognitive, and systems approaches over affective models.
- like organizational applications of psychological principles.
- may be seen by some clients as impersonal, directive, and overly analytical.
- may judge their opposite type, ISFPs, as lacking ambition and as fragile, passive, and dependent.

## Dominant Introverted Feeling Types

|  | *ISFP* | *INFP* |
|---|---|---|
| Dominant | Introverted Feeling | Introverted Feeling |
| Auxiliary | Extraverted Sensing | Extraverted Intuition |
| Tertiary | Intuition | Sensing |
| Inferior | Extraverted Thinking | Extraverted Thinking |

### ISFP and INFP Clients

Introverted Feeling types can seek help for a broad range of issues, ranging from self-doubt about competence and difficulties in dealing with external and internal stress, to a desire to find meaning and purpose in their lives. Of all the types, ISFPs are most likely to underestimate their own competence, tending to avoid leadership positions and remain in the background in group situations. In contrast, INFPs are often better able to develop and acknowledge their abilities, while at the same time suffering from doubts about their true value as human beings. Both types benefit greatly from knowing that their concerns are consistent with their personality dynamics, so they can move forward to a more positive and effective appraisal of themselves. Therapists should also be aware of the following characteristics of Introverted Feeling clients.

ISFP clients

- may seek help with low self-esteem about career competence, relationship problems, and coping with overwhelming personal and job stress.
- like focused, pragmatic approaches, as well as insight-oriented therapy that identifies life patterns and suggests alternative ways of evaluating problems.

- come across as gentle, warm, self-critical, and disparaging of their own worth.

- under stress may feel increasingly inadequate as well as uncharacteristically focused on and critical of other's failings.

- may be judged as passive, dependent, and as having inadequate or ineffective coping resources.

- benefit from supportive approaches and mild confrontation; appreciate knowing the therapist will be available when crises emerge, even after termination.

- if both dominant Feeling and auxiliary Sensing are habitually introverted, may be painfully insecure and unwilling to take even minor risks in the outer world.

## INFP clients

- readily see psychotherapy and counseling as appropriate ways to resolve personal issues and may seek therapy for depression, anxiety, and issues of self-fulfillment.

- are oriented to psychodynamic, broad explorations of personal growth and development over and beyond presenting problems.

- often present a competent, self-confident, calm demeanor and only later reveal the depth and intensity of their experienced self-doubt, despair, or sense of hopelessness.

- under stress can be initially quite critical of others and later overwhelmed by their own imagined inadequacies in all areas of life.

- may be judged as more dissatisfied, depressed, or unable to cope than they actually feel, since they are by nature questioning, ruminative, and idealistic about how they live their lives.

- benefit from a validation of their need to understand themselves and from help in clarifying and moderating their high expectations of themselves and others.

- if both dominant Feeling and auxiliary Intuition are habitually introverted, can be painfully inhibited and have great difficulty relating to people and dealing with stresses in the outside world.

### ISFP or INFP Therapists
If you are an INFP, you are highly like to enjoy doing psychodynamic, client-centered psychotherapy that emphasizes the individuality of each

client. If you are an ISFP, you will likely prefer more direct, hands-on, or behavioral approaches that use well-defined methods that yield practical results. As either type, you are likely to communicate genuine warmth, concern, and commitment to clients over and beyond what they may expect from a professional relationship. Your empathy for clients may put an extra burden on you in maintaining appropriate and effective therapeutic distance. The characteristics of Introverted Feeling therapists that are summarized below should not be taken as hard and fast rules, since therapists of the same type can be quite varied in the approaches that appeal to them.

ISFP therapists

- are infrequent in comparison to other types.
- like having clear treatment guidelines that lead to concrete results.
- establish rapport and a safe therapeutic environment by being warm and genuine.
- may be seen by some clients as too passive and accepting.
- can feel defensive with their opposite type, ENTJ, seeing them as demanding, challenging, and controlling.

INFP therapists
- are very frequent in comparison to other types.
- favor client-centered approaches that emphasize psychological and spiritual development.
- prefer long-term, psychodynamic therapy over short-term, technique-oriented, and systems methods.
- establish rapport easily, communicating genuine interest in the client's individuality.
- can see their opposites, the Extraverted Thinking types, as shallow, defensive, and overly controlling.

## Dominant Extraverted Feeling Types

|  | *ESFJ* | *ENFJ* |
|---|---|---|
| Dominant | Extraverted Feeling | Extraverted Feeling |
| Auxiliary | Introverted Sensing | Introverted Intuition |
| Tertiary | Intuition | Sensing |
| Inferior | Introverted Thinking | Introverted Thinking |

### ESFJ and ENFJ Clients

Extraverted Feeling types are by nature confident, optimistic, and trusting; they assume that there is a solution available for whatever problems occur and that the best solution can be found by identifying and seeking expert knowledge. They freely help others when asked or when they recognize someone in need. They see counseling and psychotherapy as appropriate for career advice, child-rearing issues, to assist in finding personal direction and meaning, and for psychological problems. Experiencing severe or multiple stressors may obstruct their normally effective coping resources, leading to depression, anxiety, and unfamiliar despair. Therapists should also be aware of the following characteristics of Extraverted Feeling clients.

ESFJ clients

- believe that seeking expert help through counseling and psychotherapy is appropriate and natural.
- like active involvement, support, and specific recommendations from the therapist.
- can appear overly emotional and so tenderhearted that people take advantage of them.
- may need help recognizing when their natural desire to create harmony intrudes on others' needs and desires.
- may be judged as codependent, in their natural enjoyment of helping others improve their lives.
- benefit from being encouraged to let go of some of their more burdensome responsibilities, as such a tactic can help lower their stress level.
- if both dominant Feeling and auxiliary Sensing are habitually extraverted, can try to take on everyone else's tasks and lose sight of their own sources of satisfaction and personal desires.

ENFJ clients

- are naturally attracted to counseling and psychotherapy for personal, career, and all manner of life problems.
- like any approach that stimulates their curiosity and quest for psychological and emotional connections.
- are by nature optimistic about their own and others' potential and may be reluctant to acknowledge and deal with harsh and negative realities.

- often have difficulty recognizing their own limitations, leading to stress and self-doubt.
- may be judged as insensitive to others' needs for privacy and self-determination, in their natural focus on others' limitless potential and their urge to help others develop.
- benefit from help in accepting that others' conflicts and disagreements do not necessarily need to be eliminated.
- if both dominant Feeling and auxiliary Intuition are habitually extraverted, may be overly responsive to carrying out others' projects and ideas rather than following their own intuitions.

## ESFJ or ENFJ Therapists

You probably enjoy active involvement with your clients and readily inspire confidence and hopefulness. Your enthusiasm and optimism can be very encouraging and motivating to clients, but you must be careful not to overwhelm those who prefer Introversion as they may see you as more controlling and directive than you intend. Taking a patient, less active approach to clients who seem negative and unwilling to take charge of their lives can get you to the goal faster than trying to win them over by expressing your faith in their abilities. The characteristics of Extraverted Feeling therapists that are summarized below should not be taken as hard and fast rules, since therapists of the same type can be quite varied in the approaches that appeal to them.

ESFJ therapists

- are infrequent in comparison to other types.
- prefer prescribed treatment modalities with established procedures; however, their therapeutic effectiveness is as much due to the caring and stable relationship they create as to treatment procedures.
- like frequent case consultation with other therapists and welcome their viewpoints and suggestions.
- are uncomfortable working with acting-out clients, especially when confrontation is required.
- may feel intimidated by "intellectual" clients, such as their opposite type, INTPs, and may undervalue the effectiveness of their own therapeutic approach for these clients.

ENFJ therapists

- are attracted to the field but somewhat less frequently than other Intuitive–Feeling types.
- use approaches that identify and capitalize on client strengths, actively involving clients as partners in the treatment process.
- can become bored and impatient with clients who dwell on their problems but appear to resist moving forward toward solutions.
- can be direct and confrontational in their efforts to promote client growth and development, with clients themselves as well as anyone who stands in the way of these goals.
- may feel frustrated by difficulties in establishing a therapeutic connection with INTPs and other very different types but treat this as a challenge worthy of persistence.

## Cautions

There are exceptions to the generalizations that have been made regarding characteristics of clients and therapists favoring each preference and of each of the 16 types. For example, ISTJ clients have been known to remain productively in long-term dynamically oriented therapy; INFP clients can have a deep and fruitful relationship with an ESFJ therapist. So while it is worthwhile to expect predictable type differences among clients and therapists, it is equally important to expect individual differences in the expression of type by clients and in the characteristics of therapists who are of the same type.

## Using Type in Couples Therapy

The large majority of couples benefit from an understanding of type through the MBTI. Perhaps of greatest value is that type enables the therapist to maintain genuine neutrality toward both members of the couple. Regardless of whether the therapeutic goal is to enhance, maintain, or effectively terminate a relationship, the two individuals who come out of the effort can feel understood, affirmed, and able to function both as individuals and in relationship to each other.

All type information that refers to individuals will be useful in applying type to couples, regardless of the nature of the relationships that are presented. For example, people may seek help with heterosexual or homosexual relationships, parent-adult child relationships, adult siblings, or work colleagues. The information in the preceding sections about therapist and client type differences can be readily understood and used to explain and moderate a couple's erroneous assumptions, misperceptions, and misunderstandings of each other.

The critical role of the couple's therapist in regard to typology is to "translate" the words and behaviors of each member of the couple into the language and behavior of the other. The necessity for such translation often becomes obvious to couple members during the verification and interpretation procedure described in Chapter 4. For example, a husband who has a Feeling preference may complain that his Thinking-type wife only grudgingly pays him compliments and usually only when he asks if she likes something or not. The therapist can explain to the wife that her husband does not take her approval for granted as she intends him to but rather that he needs to *hear* that she likes something he does—not just assume that if she hasn't said she doesn't like it, then she probably does like it. The therapist can also explain to the husband that it is natural for a Thinking type (who is oriented to noticing what "does not fit" or is illogical) to comment only when something is not in accord with logic and to consider that mentioning what is okay is superfluous or patronizing.

An astute couples therapist can recognize and anticipate the influence of type misunderstanding as couple members describe what is satisfying and problematic in their relationship. This often occurs before the MBTI is introduced and type language is available, so it is an excellent opportunity for counselors to develop and use everyday language to discuss type differences. Perhaps a wife is puzzled and distressed when her husband says he feels unloved and gives as evidence that his wife goes into her study and reads as soon as she gets home from work. An adult daughter may see her mother as constantly critical and disapproving, whereas the mother states that she has the greatest respect for her daughter's abilities and doesn't understand how her daughter can take her every observation and opinion as a criticism.

It is quite common in couples work to hear one or the other person make such statements as, "But I never said that" or "That's not what I meant" or "I know why you *really* did that" or "You always . . ." or "I never . . ." and many other variations on the theme of honestly hearing and understanding in ways that can be widely divergent from the statements and intents of the people involved. Type differences are rarely the only source of such disagreements, but they are almost always a contributing factor. As such, addressing type-related misunderstandings can set the stage for dealing with relationship misperceptions that are a function of a broad range of personal history and other factors.

An effective way to identify some of the sources of type-related influences is to ask each couple member to fill out the MBTI twice, the first time for themselves and a second time (at least a day later) as they think *their partner* would answer it. If the results for both are the same, issues around misattribution of motives may be involved—"I know what you are like, and you're that way because you are 'hypercritical'" (or "trying to control me," "irrational," or "stupid"). Understanding the reality of type differences helps couples come closer to interpreting words and actions from the other person's perspective; they are less likely to consider themselves to be accurate judges of what the other person means. Here the therapist's "translation skills" can be extremely helpful.

Suppose, however, that a person answering "as the other" sees the partner as a very different type than the one the partner ultimately verifies. Here the depth and complexity of misunderstanding is likely to be more challenging than merely recognizing the reality of type differences. For if you see me as someone very different from who I am, you are highly likely to misperceive my values, motives, strengths, and vulnerabilities. For example, suppose Al believes that his wife, Jill, prefers Extraversion, as he does, when in fact Jill prefers Introversion. Jill persistently complains when Al frequently invites people to dinner or asks friends to join them on vacations. Given Al's belief that Jill is "just like him," he will likely conclude that Jill doesn't like their friends. Even when Jill explains that she needs some time to herself and prefers for the two of them to be alone together, Al may interpret her statement as an excuse and denial of the truth of Jill's feelings.

The above are simple examples of the myriad ways couples can misunderstand each other and the uses to which the MBTI can be put. A comprehensive discussion of the use of type in relationship counseling is beyond the scope of this book. Several helpful resources in this area are noted

## CAUTION

### 6.1 Tips and Cautions When Using Type With Couples

- Do not use the MBTI with couples if you suspect one or both partners are likely to use the instrument merely as a weapon.

- Use the same administration and interpretation techniques as you would with individuals, if possible, talking to both couple members at the same time during all phases of the process.

- Make sure to comment on and correct statements that reflect type bias— that one attitude, function, or whole type is inherently "better" than the other.

- People are often unaware that different types express love and caring in very divergent ways, especially where a couple differs on the Thinking–Feeling dichotomy. A discussion about this in therapy can be enlightening and productive.

- Discourage couple members from using their type as an excuse for clearly objectionable behavior.

- Neither partner should be expected to bear all of the responsibility for "changing" or understanding or accommodating the other's type; compromise must be framed as an equal enterprise.

- Recognizing and accepting alternative ways of seeing and doing things comes more naturally and easily to some types than to others; be careful not to judge the more "single-minded" couple member as "the problem."

- Use the cheapest method available (probably template scoring) to score the "partner assessment" when you have couples fill the MBTI out twice; precise discrimination here is not a meaningful goal.

in the annotated bibliography. Published work, your own life experience, and your clinical work with individuals and couples will quickly add to your ability to use type effectively with couples and others with problematic relationships. Caution 6.1 lists tips and cautions to keep in mind when using type with couples.

### Using Type in Family Therapy

The same issues, techniques, values, and cautions that apply to individuals and couples are relevant when using type with families. What constitutes a

# CAUTION

## 6.2 Tips and Cautions When Using Type With Families

- Use the Murphy-Meisgeier Type Indicator for Children for family members who are approximately 8 to 12 years old, but use your judgment about which, if any, form is appropriate for children at the borders of these approximate ranges.
- Type differences often contribute meaningfully to differences in parental child-rearing philosophies.
- Be cautious in attributing differences in child-rearing styles solely to type; the way the parents themselves were raised can be equally important—by itself and in interaction with their type.
- Family members (both adults and children) often erroneously perceive another family member's type-related behavior as motivated by a desire for power and control; exploring these perceptions and clarifying everyone's motives is a critical therapeutic intervention.
- Helping family members understand each other from the other person's type perspective can have a lasting impact on reducing family strife.

family may be very broadly conceived, the range including parents, young children, adolescents, members of blended families, and adult siblings with each other and/or one or both parents. Family variables are often relevant when working with other groups of people who live with and work closely together, such as people in religious communities or close-knit work teams. As with couples, the value of type knowledge is in acknowledging and affirming each person's individuality while enabling family members to understand where each person "is coming from" in regard to values, motives, and behaviors. Material directly or indirectly relevant to applying type to family issues can be found in Ginn (1995), Meisgeier and Meisgeier (1989), Murphy (1992), and Penley and Stephens, (1994). Caution 6.2 lists tips and cautions that may be helpful when using the MBTI with families.

## Using Type With Chemically Addicted Clients

A possible association between MBTI type and addiction to alcohol and drugs has been explored over a number of years (see Quenk and Quenk,

1996, for a review of these studies). Overall, it appears that Introverts appear significantly more often in addiction treatment programs than do Extraverts. Results must be viewed with caution, however, since the prevalence of addiction by type in the general population has not been studied. Counselors and psychotherapists who treat clients in addiction settings attest to its value in helping clients better understand and accept themselves. Most important, knowledge of type differences enables therapists to take type into account in designing addiction treatment plans. (Shuck & Manfrin, 1997). Therefore all of the preceding information on type in general and client and therapist type differences in particular can be productively applied in addiction treatment. Caution 6.3 provides tips and cautions specific to using type in addiction treatment.

## CAUTION

### 6.3 Tips and Cautions When Using Type With Chemically Addicted Clients

- Clients may report a type that represents who they are when addicted, despite abstaining from chemical substances for 30 days before administration.

- A comparison of "addicted type" and verified type as reported at the end of treatment can provide client and therapist with useful insights.

- Early age of onset of addiction is likely to exacerbate client confusion or distortion regarding best fit type.

- Clients with codependency issues or early age of onset of addiction may initially answer the MBTI to reflect the counselor's type rather than their own type.

- Client-counselor type similarity is reported to be associated with greater persistence in treatment.

## Using Type With Seriously Disturbed Clients

There may be circumstances when clients in an acute state or those with more serious psychological disorders can benefit from an awareness of type differences, even if type cannot be reliably assessed. The positive and neutral language of the type approach can encourage optimism and willingness to tackle difficult problems. For example, a client may be habitu-

## CAUTION

### 6.4 Tips and Cautions For Using the MBTI With Seriously Disturbed Clients

- The MBTI can be effectively administered as a therapeutic tool specific to the client's situation.
- Neutral and positive type language can provide a vehicle for therapeutic motivation to modify problematic behaviors.
- Accurate assessment of the client's type may not be a reasonable or appropriate goal.
- Many clients can report their preferences accurately, thereby providing a useful avenue for exploring normal personality characteristics that the client may believe are pathological—for example, Introversion.

ally disorganized, scattered, and distracted to the point of immobility. If there is good reason to believe that he has a natural preference for a Perceiving rather than a Judging attitude, the therapist might suggest to the client that he may be distorting his natural tendency to "stay open to new information and a variety of experiences." Associating the behavior with "normal" personality differences can be an effective therapeutic strategy that helps calm the client and alleviate the anxiety and hopelessness that may be exacerbating symptoms.

Even where a particular client may not be able or willing to answer the MBTI, a discussion of natural type preferences can be productive. Of course, if the client is disinterested or resists, it is best not to pursue the topic. It is relatively easy for distressed clients to use any ambivalence they might have in answering the MBTI or the type they report as confirmation that they are "confused," "inferior," "crazy," or as having a wide variety of other negative attributes. Clinicians must weigh the potential benefit and harm of using the MBTI with clients on a case-by-case basis and be prepared to deal with inevitable errors in judgment. Caution 6.4 summarizes suggestions for using the MBTI with more seriously disturbed clients.

### The Relation of Type to Typical Clinical Issues

#### Learning Disabilities and Attention-Deficit Disorder

There is a large body of evidence that relates type preferences and the 16 types to educational variables (for comprehensive presentations, see DiTiberio,

1996, 1998). Information about learning disabilities and behavioral disorders is emerging but generally inconclusive, probably due to the variability of definitions, samples, and approaches involved. For clinicians who assess clients in these areas, however, type knowledge can aid in differentiating between a carefully assessed actual disorder and a perceived "possible" disorder that is a function of type bias or immature type development. For example, the normal characteristics of children who are dominant extraverted Sensing types (ESTP and ESFP) are quite similar to those that characterize attention-deficit disorder (ADD) or attention-deficit hyperactivity disorder (ADHD). Research to date indicates that these types are not overrepresented in ADD and ADHD samples (Dudding & Dudding, 1995; Meisgeier, Poillion, & Haring, 1994). However, it has been generally noted by educators familiar with type that the typical learning environment is not conducive to the natural learning styles of Sensing–Perceiving types. A useful approach when assessing learning disabilities and behavioral disorders is to consider the possibility that some of the observed behavior is a function of unmet learning style needs and/or teacher expectations that reflect type biases.

### Personality Assessment

The MBTI may be the only instrument that is administered to a client for the purpose of assessing normal personality variations, and its use as a therapeutic tool without other instruments is often appropriate. However, if the goal of assessment is differential diagnosis of a psychological disorder or general assessment of functioning for some other purpose, sole administration of the MBTI is inappropriate. The MBTI does not assess pathology and using it for such a purpose risks attributing real pathology to normal type differences. Administering the MBTI in conjunction with a variety of other instruments can provide the most inclusive assessment information for diagnosis and the development of treatment strategies.

### Assessing Effectiveness of Treatment

Because each of the 16 types is assumed to be normal and stable over the life span, any assumptions or expectations of differences in the type a person reports as an outcome of treatment are unsupportable. An appropriate treatment goal is to promote increased acceptance of, confidence in, and effective use of one's natural type. Addressing possible issues of type development is one way of accomplishing these goals. Caution 6.5 summarizes these and other clinical inferences to avoid in using the MBTI.

# CAUTION

## 6.5 Clinical Inferences to Avoid

- A client who reports a different type on a second administration has not "changed type." The results of one or the other administration *may* be a better representation of the client's best fit type.

- The numerical value of the preference clarity index does not reflect competence, maturity, access, and the like, nor do changes in this index on a second administration reflect "improvement," "growth," "more access to," or any other alteration in typological makeup.

- A slight preference clarity index on one or more preferences does not in itself justify an inference that the client is "confused," "poorly developed," "equally comfortable with both preference poles," "individuated," or "self-actualized."

- A person who has reported and verified a particular type will not necessarily "be good at" areas one might expect from that type; for example, an ISFJ may not be consistently attentive to detail or an ENFJ may be quite comfortable with confrontation.

## ✎ TEST YOURSELF ✎

1. **Clients who appear to habitually extravert both their dominant and auxiliary functions can come across as very**
   - (a) Judging.
   - (b) Extraverted.
   - (c) Intuitive.
   - (d) Feeling.

2. **Types whose natural characteristics might be erroneously seen as a evidence of a behavior disorder are**
   - (a) ESTP and ESFP.
   - (b) ISTJ and ISFJ.
   - (c) ISFP and INFP.
   - (d) ISTP and INTP.

3. **Understanding type can be helpful even before the client has taken the MBTI and has verified a type because such knowledge can aid in early establishment of**
   - (a) diagnostic impressions.
   - (b) treatment plans.
   - (c) rapport.
   - (d) all of the above.

4. **It is nearly always inappropriate to tell clients your own type.** True or False?

5. **Brain imaging studies might lead to the inference that some Introverts avoid spending time in large shopping centers because**
   - (a) they prefer buying what they need from catalogs, since they enjoy reading.
   - (b) they feel overstimulated by the sights and sounds typical of such settings.
   - (c) they like a "soft-sell" rather than a "hard-sell" approach.
   - (d) they dislike strangers.

*continued*

**6. Which of the following is generally true?**

(a) Extraverts attribute their problems to people and events in the outer world whereas Introverts attribute their problems to one or another personal attribute of their own.

(b) Extraverts tell others what they are thinking while they are thinking it; Introverts think first and tell later.

(c) Extraverts believe that Introverts are withholding or critical; Introverts believe Extraverts are intrusive or insincere.

(d) all the above

**7. Clients who are defensive and unwilling to examine their own motives usually are**

(a) ISTJs or ESTJs.

(b) poorly developed people of any type.

(c) any one of the eight Sensing types.

(d) showing many problems that are entirely unrelated to type.

**8. Clients who prefer Intuition can be expected to**

(a) challenge much of what the therapist says.

(b) be late for appointments.

(c) make inferences from what the therapist says.

(d) leave therapy after their problem is resolved.

**9. Clients with a preference for Thinking are typically *most* concerned about the therapist's**

(a) competence.

(b) warmth and expressiveness.

(c) preferred techniques.

(d) willingness to keep to a schedule.

**10. What do clients with a preference for Feeling often have difficulty in?**

(a) telling the difference between a dispassionate observation and an intended criticism

(b) telling the therapist when they disagree or have negative feelings about the therapist

(c) confronting people in their lives

(d) all the above

11. **Which of the following is generally true?**

    (a) Clients with a Judging preference experience more internal stress than clients with a Perceiving preference.

    (b) Therapists who prefer Perceiving have difficulty keeping track of appointments.

    (c) Therapists who prefer Judging often close discussion down prematurely.

    (d) None of the above is generally true.

12. **When using the MBTI with couples, it is best to administer and interpret to each person individually.** True or False?

13. **What is meant by the therapist's "translation skills" in couples therapy?**

14. **Why might ESTPs and ESFPs be seen as having behavioral problems in school?**

15. **A clearer preference clarity index on a second administration of the MBTI that occurs at the termination of therapy means**

    (a) that the therapy has been successful.

    (b) that the person has developed greater maturity in the expression of type.

    (c) that there is an obvious practice effect.

    (d) nothing, as no such conclusions can be legitimately made from preference clarity index changes.

*Answers:* 1. b; 2. a; 3. c; 4. False; 5. b; 6. d; 7. d; 8. c; 9. a; 10. d; 11. d; 12. False; 13. The ability to "explain" one person's statements in the other person's type "language"; 14. These types are naturally talkative and interactional, learning best by activity and direct action on the environment; 15. d

# ILLUSTRATIVE CASE REPORTS

The illustrative cases in this chapter synthesize the information in the preceding chapters using two different formats. The first offers a detailed presentation of one client whose type was clarified during the initial feedback sessions, for whom type was a significant therapeutic issue and tool in the conduct of psychotherapy, and for whom results from other assessment instruments confirmed and augmented type results. The second format involves the presentation of several brief illustrative cases where the Myers-Briggs Type Indicator personality inventory was the only or the primary instrument administered. The goal of this second format is to illustrate some of the ways the MBTI can be used effectively in relatively brief counseling and therapy with individuals and couples. Important factors to consider when using the MBTI with other tests and when including MBTI results in assessment reports are also included. (See Don't Forget 7.1).

## JIM

Jim's case provided an ideal illustration of the ways that the MBTI can serve both central and peripheral roles in conducting adult psychotherapy. Jim was highly motivated

---

**DON'T FORGET**

### 7.1 Tips When Including MBTI Results in a Report

- Do not state the client's MBTI type in the report, regardless of the assumed type knowledge of the recipient of the report.

- It is often effective to incorporate relevant statements from the client's type description into the report where this will aid understanding that is relevant to the referral question.

- Where relevant, temper assessments from other tests by placing them in the context of what is normal for the client's type.

for therapy and had pressing psychodynamic as well as practical issues in need of exploration. He had no prior knowledge of the MBTI and stated at the outset that he was interested in filling out any assessment instruments the therapist deemed relevant.

## Reason for Self-Referral

Jim, a 38-year-old business consultant who had been married for 2 years, stated that his two goals in seeking psychotherapy were intertwined. His primary goal was to identify a satisfying and fulfilling career and take whatever steps were necessary to achieve this, such as additional education or relevant work experience; the second goal was to examine past and present personal issues that he suspected served as impediments to reaching his first goal. He reported quite a bit of urgency in getting started resolving his problems, as he was nearing age 40.

## Background Information

Jim grew up in a small midwestern town and obtained a bachelor's degree in business administration at the local college, even though he found the courses boring and hated accounting. He had considered several majors, including art, architecture, and psychology, but he did not pursue them. Since graduation, he had held about 10 different positions in a variety of business and organizational settings, most recently as a business/management consultant for a large company. He reported that although he found consulting challenging and satisfying, he was required to travel extensively, often being home for only 1 or 2 weekends a month. That and his lack of control over his assignments were sources of great dissatisfaction. In addition, Jim recognized that his wish for career success likely required that he devote himself primarily to this arena, thereby having relatively little time for home and family, which he greatly valued. Another factor in his pursuit of appropriate work was the reality of his lifelong and severe allergies, which limited the climate in which he could comfortably live.

Jim described himself as "being on hold" and feeling stuck, ambivalent, and fearful that he would be perpetually unable to make a satisfying career decision. His longtime habit was to think about a career, such as being an architect or psychologist, quickly envision what that would be like, become enthusiastic about it, and plan (usually quite carefully and realistically) the steps involved to become an architect or psychologist. However, once he had the necessary information and a serious commitment to the plan was required, he would realize that he did not know whether this career was the "right" one—what if he made the wrong career decision and only discovered it after years of fruitless training? Jim reported that he is not self-doubting or ambivalent in the other areas of his life, such as personal relationships, buying and maintaining a house, knowing how to present himself to prospective employers, and making professional contacts. His self-doubt was only in making a commitment to one career path or, alternatively, accepting as valid a path that allows for multiple career possibilities over time. He felt that he must know the end point before he starts and could not trust that his instincts would lead him in appropriate directions.

Jim described his parents as extremely traditional and conservative socially, politically, and in their own career choices and aspirations. His father had managed a retail store in their small town for 30 years and, from Jim's point of view, was unable or unwilling to take risks that might have led to a better and more challenging work situation. His mother worked part time as a teacher's aid. In spite of their personal approach to their work worlds, however, both parents were vocal in their admiration for Jim's maternal uncle, who had achieved great professional and financial success as an attorney and entrepreneur. Jim also very much admired his uncle, who served as a role model whose success and manner were in stark contrast to what he saw as his father's passivity and lack of personal ambition.

School in his small town was not interesting, challenging, or satisfying, though Jim performed reasonably well with minimal effort. He received little encouragement to excel and did not think of himself as especially competent intellectually. He spent a good deal of time alone, finding little in common with his peers. However, he did develop a number of small business enterprises, buying and reselling various items to his schoolmates at a profit. He enjoyed both the success and money from these enterprises—and the connection it gave him to his much-admired uncle's successes. He received some positive attention for his business acumen from family and community members but also sensed discomfort from his parents when people commented on his good business sense. His parents made it clear that he was not to promote himself, as this was equivalent to arrogance, a greatly disparaged character trait. He remembered being quite confused about the "success versus boasting" issue and saw this as an early contributing factor to his low self-confidence and doubts about his decision making abilities.

## Appearance and Behavior

Jim is an attractive, soft-spoken man who looks younger than his age. His manner is friendly, considerate, and socially at ease. When describing his situation, he is serious and intense, choosing his words carefully to communicate as accurately and candidly as possible. Throughout 8 months of weekly therapy, he remained consistently open, cooperative, and nondefensive, being willing to consider, explore, and try out a wide range of psychological possibilities and proposed courses of action. He was enthusiastic about taking whatever forms of assessment were relevant and took their results quite seriously. He found the MBTI results particularly enlightening because it clarified aspects of himself that had puzzled him throughout his life.

### DON'T FORGET

#### 7.2 When the Client Has Taken the MBTI Before

If your client has previously taken the MBTI, inquire as to the following:

- When and for what purpose was the MBTI taken?
- What kind of feedback was given?
- Does the client have any incorrect assumptions about the MBTI?
- Does the client remember his or her type?

### MBTI Results

Because of his career issues, Jim was given both the MBTI and the Strong Interest Inventory® (1994) at the conclusion of the second session. Form M was not yet published when Jim began therapy and Jim filled out the long research form (Form J) of the Indicator, which provides both basic results and additional subscale information. The subscale information was peripheral to Jim's MBTI results and is not discussed here.

Prior to providing the standard administration information (see

Rapid Reference 2.1), Jim was asked if he had ever taken the MBTI or had heard anything about it. He was unfamiliar with it. Had he taken the Indicator before, the issues listed in Don't Forget 7.2 would have been pursued. With any new client to whom you introduce the MBTI, it is also important to make sure there are no misunderstandings or "holdovers" from other instruments the client may have taken. Caution 7.1 comments on these possibilities.

Jim's Form G type preferences and associated clarity of his preferences were as follows: Introversion (slight), Intuition (moderate), Thinking (clear), and Judging (slight). Note that prior to Form M, preference clarity was reported using the same

## CAUTION

### 7.1 Confusing the MBTI With Other Tests

- Clients who have taken the MMPI (Minnesota Multiphasic Personality Inventory) sometimes mistake this for the MBTI since they both start with the letter M, have a four-letter acronym, and are psychological tests. Be especially clear in explaining the differences between the two instruments.

- Clients may have taken some test whose content or variables sound similar, such as a learning-styles test or something they found in a popular book or on the Internet. Make sure there are no persisting concerns resulting from possible "look-alikes."

categories currently used in reporting Form M results. Jim's four preferences yield a reported type of INTJ.

### Initial MBTI Interpretation

In response to whether he thought he had answered the MBTI as an Extravert or Introvert, Jim correctly reported that he probably answered many items indicating both. However, he readily identified more with the overall description of Introversion, especially in regard to privacy needs and pleasure in time spent working alone and being alone. He said that as an adult he had purposefully cultivated a friendly, socially at ease approach to people, because he had found pure social relating awkward and difficult as a child and adolescent. He was now quite comfortable starting conversations with people and found himself to be genuinely interested in them. Jim's slight preference for Introversion may be due, in his case, to the fact that a fair number of E–I items deal with some aspect of social Extraversion and Introversion, the aspect of Extraversion that had apparently become a habitual part of his personality.

Jim listened particularly intently to the descriptions of Sensing and Intuition, where his reported preference for Intuition was moderate. When asked how he thought he answered, he said that he was pretty sure he answered favoring Intuition, but he felt there was something wrong with this and noted that when he considered the qualities described for Sensing perception, he found them pretty unappealing but somehow "the way you were supposed to be." When told he had indeed answered as having a preference for Intuition, he quickly surmised that both of his parents clearly preferred Sensing; he wondered whether some of his ambivalence, confusion, and distrust of himself were related to this very difference.

Jim easily identified Thinking as his judgment preference, stating that he liked logically analyzing information and aimed for objective decisions based on good evidence, though he valued harmonious relationships and tried to accommodate other people's desires when possible. In further discussion over the next several sessions, it became clear that Jim's idea of "good evidence" conformed to the characteristics of Sensing information. As a result, career contemplation that allowed free rein to exploring possibilities in the future was perceived from an exaggerated Sensing perspective—wanting to know for sure what the outcome of his plans would be. Jim's natural Intuition was thus pretty systematically discounted as a source of reliable data. Instead, he tried to base decisions on Sensing information that was unappealing and unconvincing to him. This seesaw process inevitably resulted in doubt and dissatisfaction with his decisions. Jim's natural Intuition did come out, however, but in an exaggerated and distressing form—when he found himself "spinning his wheels" about the possibilities and imagining all the ways his decisions could be wrong.

Jim's slight preference for Judging rather than Perceiving was verified in his comment that when he was focused and involved in a project he enjoyed and where he had sufficient freedom to use his talents, he was quite organized, systematic, and goal directed. However, when his confidence was low or there was insufficient structure within which he could function, he became quite distracted and unable to maintain a focus on tasks and goals. Hence, he had answered the J–P items candidly as reflecting an actual behavioral "pull" toward both poles of the dichotomy.

Jim was asked to read the INTJ description in *Introduction to Type* (Myers, 1998). He identified clearly with the characterization of this type but felt he lacked the self-confidence and conceptual clarity described. At various points later in the process of therapy, Jim recognized that perhaps he was not able to "live out" his type adequately because of his distrust and denigration of what should be his most valued and developed part, his dominant introverted Intuition.

As a check on Jim's agreement with his reported type, he was asked to spend some time at home reviewing the type descriptions for INTP, ENTP, and ENTJ—the three most likely alternatives to INTJ. In the next session he reported that although some parts of these descriptions fit, none of them resonated in the way INTJ did.

### Other Tests Administered

As a result of Jim's initial eagerness to take a variety of assessment instruments, results on several instruments were available that provided support for or enhancement of Jim's MBTI profile. (See Caution 7.2 for information on integrating other test results with the MBTI.)

#### *Strong Interest Inventory*®

Often used in conjunction with the MBTI for career counseling, the Strong Interest Inventory compares a subject's career interest patterns to those of people actually performing specific jobs or careers. Results are reported at three levels: Six General Occupational Themes; 25 Basic Interest Scales; and 211 specific Occupational Scales. The report covers the results in these three areas, as well as on four Personal Style Scales— Work Style, Learning Environment, Leadership Style, and Risk-Taking/

---

### CAUTION

#### 7.2 Integrating Other Tests with the MBTI

- Read between the lines of other tests; there may be subtle or explicit negative valuations of some normal type characteristics.

- If appropriate for a particular client, discuss positive and negative biases revealed in other tests in terms of the client's successes and difficulties in relevant life areas.

- Consider orienting therapeutic interventions around type preferences—as when Jim was shown ways to learn how to trust his dominant Intuition.

Adventure. The first page of Jim's Strong Interest Inventory report is a "snapshot" of the results, giving the clinician a quick overview of Jim's general occupational themes, the five basic interest areas on which he showed high interest, and the 10 Occupational Scales where his pattern of response was "very similar" or "similar" to individuals doing that same kind of work. Jim's snapshot revealed high interest in the Enterprising Occupation Theme, average interest in the Investigative, Artistic, and Conventional Themes, and little interest in the Realistic and Social Themes. The five basic interest scales showing high interest were Applied Arts, Law/Politics, Merchandising, Data Management, and Mathematics. Jim's Occupational Scale results showed his interests to be "very similar" to Marketing Executive, Corporate Trainer, Investment Manager, Lawyer, Actuary, College Professor, Human Resources Director, Credit Manager, and Realtor. He was "similar" to Accountant.

As was inferred from his Snapshot, Jim's career interests fit well with the kind of consulting work he was presently doing and which he apparently enjoyed. His dissatisfactions were more related to his lack of control over his work life; the amount of travel it required, which kept him away from his wife and the enjoyment of home activities; and, perhaps most important, his persistent questioning of whether this work was "right" and "the best" for him. His placement on the six General Occupational Themes, Basic Interest Areas, and the detailed results on the Occupational Scales made much sense to Jim and gave him some confirmation that he might actually be on the "right" career path in spite of his habitual distrust of his career decisions.

On the Personal Style Scales, Jim favored a work style described as "prefers to work alone; likes to work with ideas, data, or things. Accomplishes tasks by independent action or thought" (standard score = 41). His preferred Learning Environment is strongly characterized as "prefers academic environment; learns by lectures and books; willing to spend many years in school; seeks knowledge for its own sake" (standard score = 66). In terms of Leadership Style, Jim would be described as "comfortable taking charge and motivating others; enjoys initiating action; expresses opinions easily" (standard score = 62). Jim's most extreme personal style scale (standard score = 70) was on the last style, Risk Taking/Adventure, where he would be characterized as "likes adventure and risk taking; appreciates original ideas; enjoys thrilling activities; takes chances."

Jim's results on the Personal Style Scales were particularly affirming to his emerging appreciation of his Intuition. His preference for working independently meshed well with his expressive and initiating leadership style and his comfort in directing and motivating others; his attraction to originality and risk taking further confirmed his natural preference for a relatively unconstrained, intuitive approach to life.

### Adjective Check List

Respondents to the Adjective Check List (ACL; Gough & Heilbrun, 1983) are asked to describe themselves by selecting as many of the 300 adjectives listed as are relevant. Results are reported as standard scores on 37 scales that provide measures of the client's psychological needs, intellect and creativity, and ego functioning. Interpretations from both the ACL and the California Psychological Inventory (CPI) (see next section) allowed insight into characteristics that might be interacting with Jim's type, that could be seen as expressions of his individual development of his type, and that gave further insight into his overall personality.

The ACL results for Jim describe a person who acts independently of others or of social values and expectations and who is versatile, unconventional, and individualistic. However, Jim tended to see himself in an unfavorable light in a number of arenas, both in relationship to other people as well as in areas such as general self-confidence, achievement orientation, and ability to persist at tasks. The ACL results seem to mirror the self-doubt, low energy, and ambivalence Jim revealed at the beginning of therapy. An ACL profile at the completion of therapy might reveal positive changes in some of Jim's areas of difficulty, since unlike the MBTI, the ACL may legitimately suggest self-image changes attributable to psychotherapy.

### California Psychological Inventory

The third edition of the 40-year-old CPI (Gough & Bradley, 1996) provides detailed personality information organized as three structural scales that are used to create four CPI types and seven levels of actualization of each type. There are 20 Folk Concept Scales organized into four kinds of measures: (a) Poise, Self-Assurance, Interpersonal Proclivities Scales; (b) Normative Orientation and Values Scales; (c) Cognitive and Intellectual Functioning Scales; and (d) Role and Personal Style Scales. The CPI also interprets responses as

13 special purpose scales. The revised edition was normed on 6,000 people, and results are available as a profile, narrative report, or configural analysis.

Jim's narrative report provided a portrait of his functioning that corresponded well to his description of himself and to his therapist's assessment of the character and degree of his psychological adaptation. The report could also be interpreted as reflecting the interaction between Jim's INTJ type characteristics and the personality qualities assessed in the CPI. For example, Jim was described in the report as "moderately self-confident and resourceful . . . showing ingenuity and versatility in dealing with problems and a moderately strong desire for success and status" and as seeing himself as not in good health and possibly having medical problems. He was also described as "somewhat lacking in reliability and dependability . . . adapting to conventional demands with some reluctance . . . liking excitement and stimulation" and "may have considerable ability, but does not perform well in tightly defined or rule-dominated situations; in high school likely to be an underachiever; easily distracted and bored." Scales dealing with achievement orientation and intellectual efficiency described Jim as not strongly characterized at either extreme of these scales, perhaps reflecting his ambivalence regarding achieving professional status and success versus a comfortable and satisfying home life.

Results on the special purpose scales described Jim as somewhat above average in leadership potential and as very high in creative potential and desire to be innovative, while being below average in self-discipline, conscientiousness, and reliability as a worker—an observation possibly influenced by or reflective of his career ambivalence and hypothesized Sensing–Intuition "conflict." With regard to CPI type and level of attainment of that type, Jim is a "gamma" type. Gamma types are described as doubters and skeptics who at their best are innovative and insightful, with a talent for coming up with new ideas, products, or systems. INTJs are one of the MBTI types likely to come out as CPI gamma types. Jim revealed an average (4 on a scale of 1 to 7) level of self-realization or fulfillment of his gamma type, a result that is quite consistent with the level of doubt, ambivalence, and dissatisfaction he expressed in the early months of therapy.

## Jim's Form M Results

Nearly 1 year later, when psychotherapy sessions were occurring only occasionally and on an as-needed basis, Jim agreed to fill out Form M. Figure 7.1

REPORTED TYPE: INTJ

PCI: INTROVERSION I 3
INTUITION N 26
THINKING T 22
JUDGING J 5

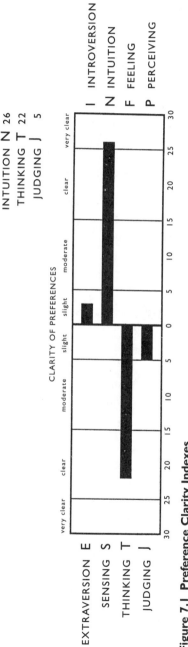

CLARITY OF PREFERENCES

EXTRAVERSION E
SENSING S
THINKING T
JUDGING J

I INTROVERSION
N INTUITION
F FEELING
P PERCEIVING

**Figure 7.1 Preference Clarity Indexes**

*Note.* Modified and reproduced by special permission of the Publisher, Consulting Psychologists Press, Inc., Palo Alto, CA 94303 from MBTI® Step I— Form M Profile for the Myers-Briggs Type Indicator. Copyright 1998 by Consulting Psychologists Press, Inc. All rights reserved. Further reproduction is prohibited without the publisher's written consent.

shows Jim's Form M profile. As shown, Jim (who was asked to answer MBTI questions as spontaneously as possible) again reported INTJ as his type. Note that his preferences for Introversion and Judging show slight preference clarity, as did the first administration that was based on Form G results, and his preference for Thinking is clear, as it was in the earlier administration. However, on Intuition Jim's preference clarity appears in the "very clear" range. This may be due to differences between Form M and Form G or to Jim's greater understanding of the Sensing–Intuition dichotomy, and/or to Jim's greater willingness to acknowledge Intuition as his preference.

## Process and Outcome of Therapy

The main typological issue in Jim's therapy was to help him gain confidence in the validity of his dominant Intuition, minimize the power of his internal "Sensing critic" that habitually overrode Intuitive information and thus allow his developed Thinking function the freedom to discriminate productively among the possibilities that emerged. During the course of therapy, Jim's therapist was alert to instances when Jim bypassed possibilities that may have been worthy of consideration and asked Jim to reconsider them. Sometimes when Jim expressed doubt about a possible course of action, the therapist agreed that it seemed like a good idea and/or engaged Jim in a discussion of what might be involved so that he could evaluate the idea from a variety of vantage points. In this way, Jim became gradually more secure and trusting of both his Intuition and Thinking. He decided to continue with his consulting work while also taking steps to increase his skills and make the necessary contacts to eventually be in greater control of his time and type of work.

Of course, there were nontypological therapeutic goals as well. These either interacted to some extent with type issues or were largely independent of them. In general, the explanatory system provided by the MBTI encouraged Jim to deal with these other problem areas and helped him discriminate appropriately between what could legitimately be attributed to his type and personality attributes that were peripheral or unrelated to type.

## USING TYPE IN BRIEF THERAPY

Various constraints on providing counseling and psychotherapy services to clients often necessitate using approaches that achieve maximum benefit in very few available sessions. The MBTI can be a very effective way of making a significant impact on an individual client or couple. In addition, an understanding of the widely different ways different types effectively utilize therapy (as described in Chapter 6) can reassure counselors and therapists who may believe that they could or should have done more for the client. The following section provides examples of such brief encounters with clients.

## Premarital Counseling

Annette and Hal decided to talk to a counselor before they got married, as both had previous unhappy marriages. Both agreed that they loved each other and were committed to making their marriage work. Hal was devoted to Annette's 3-year-old son, and Annette was delighted with their warm relationship. Hal loved talking to Annette about their plans for their future together, where they might be living 10 years from now and how he dreamed of someday leaving the large company he worked for and setting up his own small enterprise. Annette revealed (during the individual session with the counselor to obtain relevant background information) that these dreams of Hal's made her rather nervous. She was concerned about his obvious dissatisfaction with his life and feared he was not sufficiently grounded in reality. What if he made rash, precipitous decisions that could jeopardize their financial security? During his individual session, Hal acknowledged some concern about Annette's negativism about the future; she was always coming up with reasons why things wouldn't work out and seemed very reluctant to consider even the slightest risks.

The couples counselor silently hypothesized that personality differences might be influencing Hal's rhetoric and both of their concerns. The template-scorable version of the MBTI was given to the couple at the end of the first session as a routine part of premarital counseling. Hal and Annette were asked to answer for themselves as well as a second time "for each other," as described in Chapter 6. Hal and Annette brought their filled-out Indicators with them to the second session, and the counselor quickly scored all four. After a routine interpretation and verification process, Annette clearly confirmed her reported type, ISFJ, as her best fit type, and Hal readily confirmed his reported type, ENFJ. Each "accurately" answered for the other, although Hal indicated that Annette would answer *all* the E–I and S–N items in favor of Introversion and Sensing, whereas Annette believed Hal would have answered all of these items in favor of Extraversion and Intuition. In fact, though Hal and Annette were clear or very clear in their preferences on these dichotomies, neither was as clear as was reflected in the other's responses. Such answering "in the extreme" is relatively common when couple members differ on one or another preference.

Clearly, Hal and Annette were well aware of each other's type-related qualities. In discussion during the 2-hour interpretation session, both expressed their appreciation for what the other brought to the relationship. Annette enjoyed Hal's attentiveness, enthusiasm, and sociability; Hal marveled at the ease with which Annette had organized her busy work life and child-care responsibilities while creating a warm, comfortable, and well-organized home.

In discussing the ways in which their different type perspectives might be having an impact on their interpretation of each other's behavior, Annette reluctantly brought up her worry about Hal's dissatisfaction with his life and her concern that he might make rash and disastrous decisions because of his unhappiness. Hal was startled, puzzled, and somewhat hurt by Annette's revelation. "I assumed you knew that I'm very happy with my work and my life," he said. "But you know how much I love imagining what the future might be like. It's just a fantasy. It doesn't mean I'm going to up and do any of those things tomorrow! Why are you always so negative about the future, anyway?"

In the ensuing discussion, the counselor suggested that the issue of Hal's fantasies, Annette's worries, and Hal's belief that Annette had a negative attitude about the future were all due to the same type-related misinterpretations: From Annette's realistic, present-oriented, grounded point of view (as an ISFJ) there was no reason to plan for a drastically different future if you were happy in the present. She would not do such planning unless she was unhappy in the present; therefore, Hal must be unhappy and could make rash, dangerous decisions. From Hal's optimistic, future-oriented ENFJ point of view, enthusiastically imagining a different future came naturally—it was entirely independent of his present state of mind. He assumed Annette felt the same way about the positive nature of future possibilities. Therefore her reminders about everything that could go wrong with his plans, and her obvious reluctance to participate in such "dreaming," meant she was negative and pessimistic by nature.

## Comment

This way of understanding their assessments of each other made sense to Hal and Annette. They were relieved to know their fears did not accurately reflect the other's state of mind, and they agreed to make a habit of checking such concerns out rather than assuming they accurately understood each other's motivations.

## Couples Therapy That Led to Individual Therapy

Dave and his wife, Emma, participated in couples therapy about 8 years after they were married. They had found it very helpful in clarifying some of their value and style differences, especially as manifested in their opposite types: Dave verified his type as ESTP and Emma identified INFJ as her type. Dave accused Emma of being inflexible, controlling, and overly sensitive; Emma accused Dave of spreading himself too thin, not getting important tasks done in a timely fashion, and taking a lax, irresponsible attitude toward their finances—something that was of continuing concern to her. Understanding the ways in which they differed typologically ameliorated their blaming approach to each other and allowed them greater freedom to enjoy each other, though they still came to loggerheads about the same issues during especially stressful times. Over a period of several years, Dave and Emma came back to therapy for a "tune-up" about once a year. Although Emma would have liked more therapy, Dave tended to become impatient with the process; two or three sessions left him quite satisfied, grounded, and optimistic about their marriage.

On one occasion, Dave called for an appointment for himself, stating that he thought he needed some intensive individual therapy. He was uncharacteristically depressed, anxious, and confused; he felt unable to make a decision regarding an important issue in his life—whether to sell or keep the very large family farm on which he was raised and which he had recently inherited. The farm was in a distant part of the country and had been in his family for several generations. He had always dreamed of living on and working the farm and then passing it on to his own children, but his life had taken a different route. He now doubted that he would ever work the farm or live on it except for infrequent vacation visits. Supervising work on the farm from a distance would be difficult and represented potential financial difficulties that could seriously affect his family's security. This would certainly be a major issue for Emma, even if Dave had felt comfortable with this kind of uncertainty.

Toward the end of the scheduled first session, the therapist asked whether Dave had considered selling off most of the farm and keeping the main house and a small portion of the land for himself and his family. "I didn't think of that!" he exclaimed. "Actually, that could work really well. It shouldn't be hard to find one good buyer or several smaller ones. It's a fine piece of land. For me, the house and the land just around it are what I would really miss having."

"Do you want to come back next week to discuss this further?" the therapist asked. "Oh, no," he said. "I'll be fine now."

***Comment***

Dave could not come up on his own with the very simple solution his therapist suggested because of the intense emotional meaning the farm had for him. As a practical, present-oriented ESTP, it was difficult for him to imagine a compromise that would satisfy both of his conflicting desires. Thus his view of his situation was an either-or one. Seeing no way out, he became mired in his inferior introverted Intuition and tertiary Feeling functions. This stimulated overwhelming doubts, anxieties, and feelings of conflict about his deepest values. He projected his current state far into the future, quite a depressing prospect. This accounted for his uncharacteristic conviction that he needed "intensive" therapy. Note that Dave's definition of "intensive therapy" was likely quite different from that of his Intuitive therapist! Dave's one-session "cure" was genuine. His depression lifted and he was able to recognize that there was no need to take immediate action regarding the farm; he could explore other possibilities in a leisurely fashion since he now had at least one desirable option available.

## Career Counseling

At age 37, Nathan found that he lacked the necessary additional training to advance in his job as a safety engineer and recognized that he was reluctant to make a commitment to get the training. He liked the work well enough, as it satisfied his general interest in science, but he decided that if he was going to invest the time and energy in further education, perhaps some other kind of work would be more appealing. He therefore made an appointment for career counseling. As his funds were limited, the counselor sent the MBTI and Strong Interest Inventory to fill out and return. A first appointment for a 2-hour session was made after results of both instruments were available.

Early in the session, it became apparent that Nathan's sense of dissatisfaction and lack of enthusiasm with his career situation was generally true for other areas of his life, including intimate relationships, friendships, and his living situation. In interpreting and verifying the MBTI, Nathan easily affirmed his very clear preference for Introversion. He was quite pleased to discover the positive depiction of what he had previously thought of as a serious handicap. He had a similar reaction in confirming his clear preference for Intuition: He did not see this quality in himself as necessarily a handicap but felt it often distracted him from more important endeavors. Deciding between Thinking and Feeling was more difficult: Nathan's profile indicated a slight preference for Thinking, but Nathan believed that he probably really preferred a Feeling approach overall. Similarly, Nathan reported a slight preference for a Judging attitude but self-assessed as preferring Perceiving. He thought the kind of work he did might have influenced his answers on this dichotomy. Nathan thus self-assessed as an INFP rather than an INTJ, as was reported. He was asked to read the INFP description first.

Nathan was amazed at the accuracy with which the INFP type description fit him, and at the depiction of his personality as healthy and valuable. He made many connections between his vague dissatisfactions, his negative assumptions about himself, and his devaluing of his "best" characteristics. After reading alternative type descriptions, Nathan remained secure in his initial self-assessment. Nathan's Strong Interest Inventory confirmed his interest in the sciences and his attraction to psychology, which was his college minor. At the end of the initial 2-hour session, the counselor suggested that Nathan take the MBTI and Strong Interest Inventory results home and think about them. An appointment 2 weeks hence was made.

At the second session, Nathan was excited and enthusiastic by everything he had been thinking and observing about himself in the past 2 weeks. He was optimistic about the future and felt confident about his ability to pursue a satisfying career and make significant changes in his relationships and living circumstances. In fact, he had found himself persistently thinking about working with people in greater depth than was the case in his previous work.

He had already written for information about several counselor training programs and was eagerly anticipating exploring the possibilities of obtaining an advanced degree in counseling.

### Comment

The 3 hours of counseling released a good deal of energy for Nathan. This had an immediate effect on his assessment of himself, which in turn motivated him to plan and take steps to implement a desirable future. In fact, Nathan did complete a degree in counseling and has been working in the field for more than 10 years.

## Couples Therapy That Led to Individual Therapy

John and Phyllis were aged 35 and 32, respectively, and had been married for 5 years when they first sought couples therapy. As is often the case, the very things that had initially attracted them to each other were now sources of dissatisfaction and acrimony. Phyllis had initially found John's quiet depth, intellectual achievements, and his attentiveness to her extremely appealing. He was always willing to try new activities at her suggestion and seemed to enjoy them. John had liked Phyllis's vivacity, social acumen, and understanding of people. It made it easier for him to be in social situations when he didn't have to take the lead. After 5 years of marriage, however, Phyllis complained about John's lack of social skills, his never initiating interactions with friends or even family members, and his obvious displeasure whenever Phyllis accepted an invitation for them or insisted on having people over. For his part, John was acutely aware of his wife's complaints but said that Phyllis couldn't seem to understand how stressful his work life was and that he was exhausted on week nights and just wanted some silence and quiet activities on the weekends. He acknowledged that he felt very awkward and incompetent in social situations, especially when he had to play host.

The last straw for Phyllis occurred the week before the appointment. Phyllis had invited two couples over for dinner on Saturday night. John had participated minimally in the dinner conversation but then had "disappeared" into his study, muttering some excuse to the guests about having to meet a deadline at work. Phyllis tried to shrug it off while the guests were there, but when they left, she became furious at John. John was quite contrite both at the time and when Phyllis recounted the incident in the first session. "I guess I'm just incapable of being normal with people," he said. "Maybe Phyllis is right that I have a serious problem."

John and Phyllis were given the MBTI to fill out at home and bring back the next week. They were also asked to take it a second time, responding as the other would. John verified his reported type as INTJ, as did Phyllis in her "prediction" of John's responses. Both Phyllis and John agreed with Phyllis's reported type, ENFJ. Of particular note was John's initial response to the discussion of Introversion. He said that the way the therapist was describing being an Introvert made it seem normal and healthy, but that couldn't be right. He then described being frequently ridiculed by his father for being a "social imbecile" and protected by his mother, who recognized his inadequacy but assured John that it wasn't his fault. On one occasion his father told him that if John just tried harder, he could get over his shyness. His father was sure of that, because he himself had been shy as a child and adolescent and now he was really good at being direct with people and telling them off. His father had been particularly harsh when John decided to major in physics in college. He told John he would never overcome his shyness if he hid out in a laboratory.

Quite a bit of time was devoted during the 2-hour interpretation session to exploring John's conviction that Introversion was pathological. Among other things, the therapist explained that healthy Introversion was not the avoidance of people and social situations but rather a preference for and enjoyment of one's own company and that of a few other people at a time.

Two weeks later, the couple returned for their next session. "I don't understand what you did to him," exclaimed Phyllis. "I thought you had convinced him that being an Introvert was okay, but you know what? A few days after we saw you, he invited two couples he barely knew to come over for dinner on Friday, and when they came, he had a wonderful time and hardly left the room! I just don't understand. I love it that he did that, but I don't get it!"

### Comment

What the therapist explained in response to Phyllis's question was that most likely John had become aware that a formerly despised and mortifying part of him was actually normal and acceptable. He no longer had to hide this from others, so he felt free to try out being sociable as an Introvert rather than assuming he had to behave like an Extravert. His eagerness to try out his new-found view of himself certainly startled and confused his wife but greatly alleviated this source of stress in their marriage.

As might be expected, there were a number of other aspects of John's self-image that had become attached to his pathological interpretation of Introversion. There were also other unresolved issues in his relationship to his parents, especially his father. After several more sessions as a couple, John and the therapist agreed to continue therapy with John as an individual.

## 🐾 TEST YOURSELF 🐾

1. **Why is it important to check out a client's prior knowledge of the MBTI?**
   (a) The client may have been given incorrect feedback previously.
   (b) The client may be confusing the MBTI with the MMPI.
   (c) The client may have taken an MBTI "look-alike" rather than the MBTI.
   (d) all of the above

2. **Other assessment tools must always be used for the MBTI to be interpreted successfully.** True or False?

3. **Most other assessment instruments contain a great deal of type bias, so their results should be generally discounted.** True or False?

4. **What is the main reason a client's MBTI type should not be mentioned in a report?**
   (a) The type could change on a subsequent administration.
   (b) Revealing someone's type is unethical.
   (c) Readers of the report will likely vary considerably in their knowledge and understanding of the MBTI.
   (d) all of the above

5. **Why might an ESTJ become uncontrollably tearful and an INFP become very efficient in response to the breakup of an intimate relationship?**

*Answers:* 1. d; 2. False; 3. False; 4. c; 5. The ESTJ may be in the grip of inferior, exaggerated Introverted Feeling, expressed as emotionalism; the INFP may be expressing inferior Extraverted Thinking, thus acting like an exaggerated ESTJ.

# Appendix A

## Self-Selection Ratio Type Table: Counselors

The type table shown in this appendix is an example of a standard way of studying and presenting type information for a sample of interest. The counselors included in this table are a composite made up of 9 separate type tables that are included in the *Atlas of Type Tables* (MacDaid, McCaulley, & Kainz, 1986). *Note that the data reported in this appendix are for Form G of the MBTI.* All of the samples are samples of convenience; that is, they were contributed by various researchers or practitioners who sent in type tables to the Center for Applications of Psychological Type. The compilation is made up of the following kinds of counselors. (The Atlas type table number and page where it appears in the Atlas is provided.)

Counselors: General (#8623174; page 201)
Counselors: Rehabilitation (#8629451; page 203)
Counselors: Vocational and Educational (#8629450; page 207)
Counselors: Runaway Youth (#8623170; page 204)
Counselors: School (#8623175; page 205)
Counselors: Suicide and Crisis (#8701301; page 206)
Counselors: Social Workers (#8629449; page 209)
Counselors: Psychologists (#8629455; page 211)
Social Scientists: (#8629456; page 212)

## LAYOUT OF THE TYPE TABLE

The layout of type tables is a logical array of the types that permits quick recognition of likely self-selection factors in the sample shown. Note that the two top rows of the table show the eight types who prefer Introversion and the two bottom rows the eight types who prefer Extraversion. The two left-hand columns show the 8 types who prefer Sensing and the two right-hand columns the 8 types preferring Intuition. In the two outer columns are the 8 Thinking types and in the two inner columns are the 8 Feeling types. The 8

Judging types occupy the top and bottom two rows and the 8 Perceiving types are in the two inner rows. With a little experience in looking at type table data, one can also readily recognize specific combinations of two preferences, which can help in the interpretation of which typological factors might be influencing the distribution of types in the sample. For example, while it is quite apparent that in the counselor sample Intuitive types are much more frequent than Sensing types, one can also see that among the Intuitive types, the four NF types (INFJ, INFP, ENFP, ENFJ) are the most frequent. Similarly, among the Sensing types, the four SP types (ISTP, ISFP, ESTP, ESFP) are the least represented. Valuable descriptive and research information about the characteristics of people who share two type preferences can be found in Myers et al. (1998, pp. 38–63).

## HOW TO INTERPRET THE DATA IN THE TYPE TABLE

As indicated under the title of the type table, the total sample size for the combined sample of counselors is 3,246. The base population used for comparison was a combined sample of male and female college graduates, since by and large counselors need to have a college degree as a minimum educational qualification. This base population consisted of 8,982 individuals, and, as indicated on the table, the base sample and research sample were independent of each other. These data permit us (granting the limitations of samples of convenience) to answer the question, "How do college graduates who become counselors differ in type from college graduates in general?" Each cell of the type table shows the sample size for that type and the associated percent of the total sample. The selection ratio information appears as I, for Index of Attraction, and asterisks beside the index show significance levels resulting from Chi Square analysis. Recall from Chapter 1 that an index greater than 1 indicates overrepresentation of the type relative to the base population, an index of less than 1 shows underrepresentation, and an index near 0 is the expected representation, assuming type is not influencing selection into the group. To the right of the type table are the same data for each preference of each dichotomy individually, by two-letter combinations, and by dominant functions.

By whole type, INFJ, INFP, ENFP, and ENFJ are more attracted to counseling as an occupation than college graduates in general; ISTJ, ISFJ, INTJ,

ISTP, ESTP, ESFP, ESTJ, and ENTJ are underrepresented. It is interesting to speculate on the observation that people who counsel and those who are attracted to being counseled (see Chapter 6) tend to be quite similar in type. Further, the predominant types who choose counseling as a career are likely to be providing services to many people who are quite different from them; among the kinds of counselors included in this sample are several whose clients are referred by others rather than seeking counseling on their own.

Looked at according to each dichotomy, the table shows that Extraverts, Intuitives, Feeling types, and Perceiving types are overrepresented and Introverts, Sensing types, Thinking types, and Judging types are underrepresented. The overrepresentation of Extraverts in this sample is likely due to the broad range of counseling endeavors included. It would be reasonable to expect that Introverts would predominant in more individual-oriented therapies and Extraverts in more group-focused therapies. By dominant function, those with dominant Intuition and those with dominant Feeling are overrepresented, while those with dominant Sensing and those with dominant Thinking are underrepresented.

Readers of this book will find no surprises in the data in this type table. By and large, the relative attractiveness of the counseling field to different types conforms to what we would expect based on type theory. This type table and hundreds of others provide evidence for the construct validity of the MBTI, as well as providing counselors and other professionals with useful information for helping their clients.

## Table A-1.   Counselors Compared with College Graduates (*N* = 3246)

| ISTJ | ISFJ | INFJ | INTJ |
|---|---|---|---|
| N = 181 | N = 175 | N = 216 | N = 168 |
| % = 5.58 | % = 5.39 | % = 6.65 | % = 5.18 |
| I = 0.40*** | I = 0.84* | I = 1.27** | I = 0.67*** |

| ISTP | ISFP | INFP | INTP |
|---|---|---|---|
| N = 45 | N = 83 | N = 428 | N = 170 |
| % = 1.39 | % = 2.56 | % = 13.19 | % = 5.24 |
| I = 0.59** | I = 1.00 | I = 2.14*** | I = 1.13 |

| ESTP | ESFP | ENFP | ENTP |
|---|---|---|---|
| N = 38 | N = 103 | N = 583 | N = 159 |
| % = 1.17 | % = 3.17 | % = 17.96 | % = 4.90 |
| I = 0.67* | I = 1.35* | I = 2.25*** | I = 0.99 |

| ESTJ | ESFJ | ENFJ | ENTJ |
|---|---|---|---|
| N = 180 | N = 187 | N = 314 | N = 216 |
| % = 5.55 | % = 5.76 | % = 9.67 | % = 6.65 |
| I = 0.46*** | I = 0.89 | I = 1.55*** | I = 0.72*** |

|  | N | % | I |
|---|---|---|---|
| E | 1780 | 54.84 | 1.07*** |
| I | 1466 | 45.16 | 0.92*** |
| S | 992 | 30.56 | 0.64*** |
| N | 2254 | 69.44 | 1.33*** |
| T | 1157 | 35.64 | 0.63*** |
| F | 2089 | 64.36 | 1.48*** |
| J | 1637 | 50.43 | 0.75*** |
| P | 1609 | 49.57 | 1.52*** |
| IJ | 740 | 22.80 | 0.68*** |
| IP | 726 | 22.37 | 1.43*** |
| EP | 883 | 27.20 | 1.60*** |
| EJ | 897 | 27.63 | 0.81*** |
| ST | 444 | 13.68 | 0.46*** |
| SF | 548 | 16.88 | 0.95 |
| NF | 1541 | 47.47 | 1.85*** |
| NT | 713 | 21.97 | 0.83*** |
| SJ | 723 | 22.27 | 0.57*** |
| SP | 269 | 8.29 | 0.92 |
| NP | 1340 | 41.28 | 1.74*** |
| NJ | 914 | 28.16 | 0.99 |
| TJ | 745 | 22.95 | 0.53*** |
| TP | 412 | 12.69 | 0.93 |
| FP | 1197 | 36.88 | 1.94*** |
| FJ | 892 | 27.48 | 1.13*** |
| IN | 982 | 30.25 | 1.27*** |
| EN | 1272 | 39.19 | 1.38*** |
| IS | 484 | 14.91 | 0.59*** |
| ES | 508 | 15.65 | 0.69*** |
| Sdom | 497 | 15.31 | 0.63*** |
| Ndom | 1126 | 34.69 | 1.34*** |
| Tdom | 611 | 18.82 | 0.67*** |
| Fdom | 1012 | 31.18 | 1.45*** |

*Note.* ■ = 1% of sample; *<.05; **<.01; ***<.001. Base total *N* = 8,982. Groups are independent. Calculated values of Chi square *or* Fisher's exact probability. Data compiled and analyzed by Center for Applications of Psychological Type. Modified and reproduced by permission of Center for Applications of Psychological Type, Gainesville, FL. 32609. From G. P. MacDaid, M. H. McCaulley, & R. I. Kainz, *Atlas of Type Tables.* Copyright 1986 by Center for Applications of Psychological Type. All rights reserved.

# Appendix B

## Specialized MBTI Reports: Form M and Extended Forms

| Report | Form | Description |
|---|---|---|
| Interpretive Report for Organizations | M | Identifies strengths, leadership style, preferred work environments |
| Team Report | M | Identifies a group's type, its strengths and weaknesses, problem-solving styles, and management styles |
| Leadership Report | M | Explores client leadership style with combined results of the MBTI and FIRO-B |
| MBTI Career Report | M | Identifies occupational matches with types and gives strategies to improve job satisfaction |
| Strong & MBTI Career Report | M | Integrates Strong Interest Inventory® results with MBTI type to enhance career counselor effectiveness in guiding client career exploration |
| Strong & MBTI Entrepreneur Report | M | A career development report combining Strong and MBTI results in relation to a client's entrepreneurial potential |
| MBTI Expanded Profile | K (131 items) | 3-page profile giving individualized results on 20 subscales of the 4 MBTI dichotomies |
| Expanded Interpretive Report | K (131 items) | 24-page report giving detailed descriptions of the meaning of individualized results on 20 subscales in relation to 4-letter type |
| Type Differentiation Indicator | J (290 items) Level C qualification | For use in clinical and research settings to identify potential strengths and impediments in client development and expression of type |

# Appendix C

## Major Organizations Concerned with Psychological Type

Association for Psychological Type (APT). A nonprofit membership organization bringing together professionals from many disciplines, including counselors and psychotherapists, career counselors, educators, management consultants, multicultural specialists, researchers, and a variety of other individuals who use type and the MBTI in their work. The association offers basic and advanced training to professionals in all relevant disciplines, enabling professionals who are not educationally qualified to purchase psychological tests the opportunity to obtain qualification through APT training. A biennial international conference provides workshops, seminars, research, and application offerings. Biennial regional conferences are held in the alternate year, and many local chapters within each region offer educational programs throughout the year. In addition, members receive quarterly issues of the *Journal of Psychological Type,* a refereed journal containing research on all aspects of type and the MBTI. Members also receive 8 issues of *The Bulletin of Psychological Type,* a newsletter with brief articles, reviews, and announcements of type-related occurrences.

Further information about the association and back issues of the *Journal of Psychological Type* can be obtained from:

Association for Psychological Type
9140 Ward Parkway
Kansas City, MO 64114
816-444-3500

Center for Applications of Psychological Type (CAPT). Originally created by Isabel Briggs Myers and Mary H. McCaulley in 1975, CAPT is a nonprofit center that maintains an extensive MBTI databank, conducts research on the MBTI, provides research consultation and a continuously updated bibliography of work on the MBTI, and houses a complete library of literature on the subject. In addition, CAPT conducts basic and advanced professional training and publishes or distributes books and a wide variety of MBTI training materials. The center also sponsors annual or biennial conferences on type and education, type and leadership, and clinical applications of the MBTI. Further information can be obtained from:

Center for Applications of Psychological Type
2815 NW 13th Street
Suite 401
Gainesville, FL 32609
800-777-CAPT

Myers & Briggs Foundation, Inc. Formerly known as the Isabel Briggs Myers Memorial Fund, the nonprofit foundation is devoted to encouraging and supporting the understanding of individual differences in healthy personality by supporting research, theoretical, and educational endeavors that focus on psychological type. The foundation is sustained entirely by contributions and grants. One of its activities is the awarding of the Isabel Briggs Myers Memorial Research Award, given biennially for the best published or unpublished research on type performed by students or professionals. The list of awards given by the foundation that appears in Appendix D is indicative of the breadth of research endeavors that have been stimulated by the MBTI. Additional information can be obtained from:

Myers & Briggs Foundation
11215 Oakleaf Drive
Silver Spring, MD 20901-1381
301-593-8995

# Appendix D

**Recipients and Titles of Isabel Briggs Myers Memorial Research Awards, 1981–1999**

**1981**

Ruth G. Sherman

Typology and problems in intimate relationships. *Journal of Psychological Type, 4,* 4–23.

Philip Jacoby

Psychological types and career success in the accounting profession. *Journal of Psychological Type, 4,* 24–37.

**1983**

Nancy G. McCarley

Test-retest reliabilities of scales and subscales of the Myers-Briggs Type Indicator and of criteria for clinical interpretive hypotheses involving them. *Journal of Psychological Type, 6,* 24–36.

Flavil R. Yeakley, Jr.

Implications of communication style research for psychological type theory. *Journal of Psychological Type, 6,* 4–23.

**1985**

Anna-Maria Garden

The effect of Jungian type on burnout. *Journal of Psychological Type, 10,* 3–10.

Lou E. Hicks

Conceptual and empirical analysis of some assumptions of an explicitly typological theory. *Journal of Personality and Social Psychology, 46,* 1118–1131.

**1987**

Nancy G. McCarley

The perceived accuracy of elements of the 16 type descriptions of Myers and Keirsey among men and women. *Journal of Psychological Type, 11,* 2–29.

Elizabeth Murphy

The development of the Murphy-Meisgeier Type Indicator for Children. *Journal of Psychological Type, 13,* 15–22.

**1989**

Colleen Hester

The effects of personality style configurations and logical reasoning scores on academic achievement in computer science. *Journal of Psychological Type, 18,* 43–49.

Martha A. Wilson

Differences in brain electrical activity patterns between introverted and extraverted adults. *Journal of Psychological Type, 18,* 14–23.

**1991**

Eduardo Casas

The development of the French version of the MBTI in Canada and in France. *Journal of Psychological Type, 20,* 3–15.

Wayne D. Mitchell

A test of type theory using the TDI. *Journal of Psychological Type, 22,* 15–26.

**1993**

Kim K. Metcalf
Martha A. Wilson

Improving the efficacy of on-campus laboratory experiences using the Myers-Briggs Type Indicator. *Journal of Research and Development in Education, 27,* 2, 89–101.

Angileen P. Gilbert

A comparison of results of the Murphy-Meisgeier Type Indicator For Children (MMTIC) and the MBTI among students in grades 6-10. Not yet published.

Sandra B. Goldman

Psychological type and drug choice. *Journal of Psychological Type, 27,* 27–31.

**1995**

Roger R. Pearman
John D. Fleenor

Differences in observed and self-reported qualities of psychological types. *Journal of Psychological Type, 39,* 3–17.

Nancy S. Marioles
Donald P. Strickert
Allen P. Hammer

Attraction, satisfaction, and psychological types of couples. *Journal of Psychological Type, 36,* 16–27.

**1997**

Gerald D. Otis

Rebelliousness and psychological distress in a sample of introverted veterans. *Journal of Psychological Type, 40,* 20–30.

**1999**

Jean Reid

The relationships among personality type, coping strategies, and burnout in elementary teachers. Not yet published.

# References

Association for Psychological Type. (1992). Ethical principles. In *Membership directory, Association for Psychological Type,* Kansas City, MO.

Brock, S. A. (1994). *Using type in selling.* Palo Alto, CA: Consulting Psychologists Press.

CAPT Bibliography for the Myers-Briggs Type Indicator Diskette. (1999). Gainesville, FL: Center for Applications of Psychological Type.

Center for Applications of Psychological Type. (1995). *Profile of your MBTI results.* Gainesville, FL: Center for Applications of Psychological Type.

Corlett, E. S., & Millner, N. B. (1993). *Navigating midlife: Using typology as a guide.* Palo Alto, CA: Davies-Black.

Costa, P. Y., & McCrae, R. R. (1985). *The NEO personality inventory manual,* Odessa, FL: Psychological Assessment Resources.

DiTiberio, J. K. (1996). Education, learning styles, and cognitive styles. In A. L. Hammer (Ed.), *MBTI Applications: A decade of research on the Myers-Briggs Type Indicator* (pp. 123–166). Palo Alto, CA: Consulting Psychologists Press.

DiTiberio, J. K. (1998). Uses of type in education. In Myers, et al., *MBTI Manual: A guide to the development and use of the Myers-Briggs Type Indicator.* (p. 259). Palo Alto, CA: Consulting Psychologists Press.

DiTiberio, J. K., & Hammer, A. L. (1993). *Introduction to type in college.* Palo Alto, CA: Consulting Psychologists Press.

Dudding, B. A., & Dudding, G. S. (1995). Exploring psychological type in children with Attention Deficit-Hyperactivity Disorder (ADHD) and Attention Deficit Disorder (ADD). In *Proceedings: XI International Conference, Association for Psychological Type,* Kansas City, Mo. July 11–16. Pgs. 19–22.

Ginn, C. W. (1995). *Families: Using type to enhance mutual understanding.* Gainesville, FL: Center for Applications of Psychological Type.

Gough, H. G., & Bradley, P. (1996). *CPI manual* (3rd ed.). Palo Alto, CA: Consulting Psychologists Press.

Gough, H. G., & Heilbrun, A. B. (1983). *The Adjective Check List manual.* Palo Alto, CA: Consulting Psychologists Press.

Hammer, A. L. (1993). *Introduction to type and careers.* Palo Alto, CA: Consulting Psychologists Press.

Hammer, A. L. (1996). *MBTI applications: A decade of research on the Myers-Briggs Type Indicator.* Palo Alto, CA: Consulting Psychologists Press.

Hirsh, S. K. (1992). *Introduction to type and teams.* Palo Alto, CA: Consulting Psychologists Press.

Hirsh, S. K., & Kummerow, J. M. (1998). *Introduction to type in organizations* (3rd ed.) Palo Alto, CA: Consulting Psychologists Press.

Jones, J. H., & Sherman, R. G. (1997). *Intimacy and type: A practical guide for improving relationships.* Gainesville, FL: Center for Applications of Psychological Type.

Jung, C. G. (1954). The psychology of the transference. In *Collected works* (Vol. 16, R. F. C. Hull, Trans.). Princeton, NJ: Princeton University Press.

Jung, C. G. (1921/1971). Psychological types. *Collected works* (Vol. 6, R. F. C. Hull, Trans.). Princeton, NJ: Princeton University Press.

Kummerow, J. M. (1986). *Verifying your type preferences.* Gainesville, FL: Center for Applications of Psychological Type.

Lawrence, G., & Martin, C. R. (1996). *Profile of your MBTI results* [Handout]. Gainesville, FL: Center for the Application of Psychological Type.

McCaulley, M. H. (1985). The selection ratio type table: A research strategy for comparing type distributions. *Journal of Psychological Type, 10,* 46–56.

McCrae, R. R., & Costa, P. T., Jr. (1989). Reinterpreting the *Myers-Briggs Type Indicator* from the perspective of the five-factor model of personality. *Journal of Personality, 57,* 17–40.

Meisgeier, C. H., & Meisgeier, C. (1989). *A parent's guide to type.* Gainesville, FL: Center for Applications of Psychological Type.

Meisgeier, C. H., Poillion, M. J., & Haring, K. (1994). The relation between ADHD and Jungian psychological type: Commonality in Jungian psychological type preferences among students with Attention Deficit-Hyperactivity Disorder. *Proceedings: Orchestrating Educational Change in the '90s—The Role of Psychological Type,* 11–22.

Millon, T. (1994). *Millon Index of Personality Styles manual.* San Antonio, TX: The Psychological Corporation.

Mitchell, W. D. (with Quenk, N. L., & Kummerow, J. M.). (1999). *MBTI Step II: A description of the subscales.* Palo Alto, CA: Consulting Psychologists Press.

Murphy, E. (1992). *The developing child: Using Jungian type to understand children.* Palo Alto, CA: Consulting Psychologists Press.

Murphy, E. (1998, August). Row, row, row your boat: T–F differences across the ages. Keynote Address presented at the Association for Psychological Type, Southeast Regional Conference, New Orleans, LA.

Murphy, E., & Meisgeier, C. H. (1987). *Murphy-Meisgeier Type Indicator for Children manual.* Palo Alto, CA: Consulting Psychologists Press.

Myers, I. B. (1962). *Manual: The Myers-Briggs Type Indicator.* Princeton, NJ: Educational Testing Service.

Myers, I. B. (with Kirby, L. K., & Myers, K. D.). (1998). *Introduction to type* (6th ed.). Palo Alto, CA: Consulting Psychologists Press.

Myers, I. B., & McCaulley, M. H. (1985). *Manual: A guide to the development and use of the Myers-Briggs Type Indicator.* (2nd ed.). Palo Alto, CA: Davies-Black.

Myers, I. B., McCaulley, M. H., Quenk, N. L., & Hammer, A. L. (1998). *MBTI manual: A guide to the development and use of the Myers-Briggs Type Indicator.* (3rd ed.). Palo Alto, CA: Consulting Psychologists Press.

Myers, K. D., & Kirby, L. K. (1994). *Introduction to type dynamics and development: Exploring the next level of type.* Palo Alto, CA: Consulting Psychologists Press.

Pearman, R. (1993). Einstein's injunction. *Bulletin of Psychological Type, 16,* 1.

Penley, J. P., & Stephens, D. W. (1994). *Handbook: Understanding your personality type in mothering.* Gainesville, FL: Center for Application for Psychological Type.

Quenk, N. L. (1993). *Beside ourselves: Our hidden personality in everyday life.* Palo Alto, CA: Davies-Black.

Quenk, N. L. (1996). *In the grip: Our hidden personality.* Palo Alto, CA: Consulting Psychologists Press.

Quenk, N. L., & Kummerow, J. M. (1996). *MBTI Expanded Interpretive Report: Form K.* Palo Alto, CA: Consulting Psychologists Press.

Quenk, N. L., & Quenk, A. T. (1996). Counseling and psychotherapy. In A. L. Hammer (Ed.), *MBTI applications: A decade of research on the Myers-Briggs Type Indicator* (pp. 105–122). Palo Alto, CA: Consulting Psychologists Press.

Saunders, D. R. (1987). *Type Differentiation Indicator manual.* Palo Alto, CA: Consulting Psychologists Press.

Saunders, D. R. (1989). *MBTI Expanded Analysis Report manual.* Palo Alto, CA: Consulting Psychologists Press.

Strong Interest Inventory. (1994). Palo Alto, CA: Consulting Psychologists Press.

Shuck, J., & Manfrin, C. (1997). *Client verification of reported type at onset and after six months of continuous treatment in an abstinence-based chemical dependency treatment program.* Unpublished manuscript.

Wheelwright, J. B., Wheelwright, J. H., & Buehler, H. A. (1964). *Jungian type survey: The Gray-Wheelwright Test* (6th ed.). San Francisco: Society of Jungian Analysts of Northern California.

# Annotated Bibliography

Barger, N. J., & Kirby, L. K. (1995). *The challenge of change in organizations: Helping employees thrive in the new frontier.* Palo Alto, CA: Davies-Black.

*The impact of type on the way people deal with change and transition in the workplace is thoroughly explained in this book. It contains many insights that counselors and therapists can incorporate into their work with clients who are dealing with change in their work lives. The practical suggestions included that can ease the process for different types are firmly grounded in type theory and supported by the extensive experience of the authors. Organizational consultants, executive coaches, managers, and employees at all levels will find enlightening understanding of their own and others' reactions to change. The authors provide convincing evidence that different types define workplace change in different ways, and have different motives, goals, and needs when it comes to accepting and embracing transitions in their work lives.*

Corlett, E. S., & Millner, N. B. (1993). *Navigating midlife: Using typology as a guide.* Palo Alto, CA: Davies-Black.

*This book focuses on important developments in one's type that often accompany midlife transitions, providing helpful information and insight for clients and therapists who are dealing with midlife issues. Jung's theory claims that an individual's type develops and become more inclusive of less-preferred functions and attitudes throughout life. Both therapists and clients can benefit from understanding the predictable ways in which their interests, desires, and expressions of personality may change, sometimes dramatically, during the important midlife stage of our lives. The authors report results of empirical and observational research that show the type-consistent ways that each of the 16 types is likely to experience and react to this important part of their lives. Many examples and illustrations support the theory-based dynamic explanations.*

Fitzgerald, C., & Kirby, L. K. (Eds.). (1997). *Developing leaders: Research and applications in psychological type and leadership development.* Palo Alto, CA: Davies-Black.

*The seventeen contributed chapters in this book cover a wide range of research and professional experience with the MBTI in relation to leadership in organizations as a general issue, in teams, and in leadership development. A number of the chapters report studies that used the MBTI in conjunction with other assessment instruments, including the California Psychological Inventory (CPI), the FIRO-B (Fundamental Interpersonal Relations Orientation–Behavior), 360-degree management feedback instruments, and the SYMLOG (Systematic Multiple-Level Observation of Groups). Other chapters include a review and critique of the research literature on psychological type and leadership; type, leadership, and change; decision-making styles; a comparative analysis of manager profiles and the MBTI; type dynamics and leadership development; using the MBTI with management simulations; "STJ's and Change" (an especially insightful chapter on the perceived "resistance" of these types to workplace change); and strategies for enhancing leader communication through psychological type. Much of the information in the various chapters will be useful to psychologists and others who work with organizations and to clinicians who see clients who are in organizations that focus on developing leaders and working under leaders in the workplace.*

Hammer, A. L. (Ed.). (1996). *MBTI applications: A decade of research on the Myers-Briggs Type Indicator.* Palo Alto, CA: Consulting Psychologists Press.

*In addition to chapters covering reliability and validity evidence for the MBTI during the decade following publication of the second edition of the MBTI manual (1985), this edited volume contains 9 chapters detailing research done during that decade in 7 application areas: Career Management and Counseling; Management and Leadership; Teams; Counseling and Psychotherapy; Education, Learning Styles and Cognitive Styles; Multicultural Applications; and Health, Stress, and Coping. Practitioners who apply type in one or more of these areas will find a wealth of research information relevant to their field. Each chapter concludes with suggestions for further research, which will be of interest to those wishing to undertake research in specific application areas.*

Hirsh, S. A., & Kummerow, J. M. (1998). *Introduction to type in organizations.* Palo Alto, CA: Consulting Psychologists Press.

*The current, third edition of this booklet is useful for applications of type in organizational settings or in any context where the focus is on the ways that people differ from each other in the workplace. In addition to discussions of various groupings of type preferences, it describes each of the 16 types with regard to contribution to the organization, leadership style, preferred learning style, potential pitfalls, problem-solving approach, preferred work environments, and suggestions for development. The booklet can be particularly useful for counselors and psychotherapists who have clients grappling with demands of the workplace that force them to function using their nonpreferences, since the type descriptions present each type as making valuable and legitimate contributions to organizations.*

Lawrence, G. (1993). *People types and tiger stripes* (3rd ed.). Gainesville, FL: Center for Applications of Psychological Type.

*First published in 1979, this current edition is the third revision. It is a classic work on type and education, covering research and practical applications in educational settings at all levels. Included are discussions of type, motivation, and learning styles, a summary of the research literature in these areas, and a discussion of the learning preferences of each of the types; an insightful chapter on differing teaching styles and how teachers can modify their preferred approach to accommodate learners of all types; curriculum planning and curriculum reform; how to avoid the kind of stereotyping that often occurs in education when type differences are not understood; the role of type development in education and how to introduce the MBTI into educational organizations.*

Marioles, N. S., Strickert, D. P., & Hammer, A. L. (1996). Attraction, satisfaction, and psychological types of couples. *Journal of Psychological Type, 36,* 16–27.

*An award-winning report of the initial research results of an ongoing study of 426 married and premarital couples. It is important because marriage patterns and satisfaction of couple members were analyzed at the level of whole type rather than individual preferences. In addition, Form J, the lengthy research form of the MBTI, was used, which enabled researchers to analyze couples variables at the level of the 27 subscales elicited by this MBTI form. The research reported contradicts the popular notion that "opposites attract." Several earlier studies by other researchers (including one by Isabel Myers that is included in her book,* Gifts Differing*) had also found no evidence of opposite types predominating among couples. Satisfaction with intimate relationships was explored using several measures, one of which resulted in an index that reflects discrepancies in satisfaction between the partners in a couple. Other studies of indexes of attraction and satisfaction in relation to the type mix of couples were also developed and analyzed.*

Mitchell, W. D. (with Quenk, N. L., & Kummerow, J. M.). (1999). *MBTI Step II: A description of the subscales.* Palo Alto, CA: Consulting Psychologists Press.

*Although intended for users of the extended form of the Indicator known as MBTI Step II, Mitchell's comprehensive, detailed descriptions of each of the 5 subscales that are component parts of the dichotomies (20 subscales in all) are an excellent way for users of Form M to achieve depth of understanding of the multifaceted nature of type constructs. Knowing about five of the parts that contribute to an underlying type preference can help in the interpretation and verification process by suggesting examples to use during an interpretation session. Subscale information also promotes understanding of some of the individual differences in expression of type that clients may spontaneously reveal. For professionals wishing to use Step II with their clients, the booklet provides information about the underlying basis of the Step II scoring system, differences between the scoring of Step I (the 4-letter type resulting from Form M administration) and the Step II scoring system, and definitions of indexes and comparative normative groups.*

Murphy, E. (1992). *The developing child: Using Jungian type to understand children.* Palo Alto, CA: Consulting Psychologists Press.

*This is a classic work by the coauthor of the Murphy-Meisgeier Type Indicator for Children. It focuses on type as it develops in children and the ways it influences relationships within the family, at school, and with peers. In addition to its relevance to education and child-rearing, it can provide insights to counselors and psychotherapists who work with adults who are trying to better understand their experiences within their family. Understanding the effects of type differences in developing children does not require administration of a type assessment instrument like the Murphy-Meisgeier Type Indicator for Children (MMTIC). Parents, teachers, and professionals who work with them will readily recognize and be able to identify the nature of the differences this book illuminates.*

Myers, I. B. (with Kirby, L. K., & Myers, K. D.). (1998). *Introduction to type* (6th ed.). Palo Alto, CA: Consulting Psychologists Press.

*This 40-page booklet is the best brief resource on the MBTI that is available. It's principle use is as a resource every client takes away from an interpretation/verification session. The 16 type descriptions are faithful to Myers's original (1962) text and enhanced by empirical research and practitioner experience. Each type description includes sections on the type at their best, their basic characteristics, how others may see them, and potential areas for growth. There are additional sections in the booklet covering type dynamics and development, discussions of the common characteristics of people who share particular combinations of preferences, ethical guidelines in using type, applications of type in a number of settings, and suggestions for further reading. There is also an especially useful description of how to use all four functions (Sensing, Intuition, Thinking, and Feeling) in decision making. Anyone who interprets the MBTI to clients and applies type in any setting will want to be thoroughly familiar with the contents of this booklet as well as provide a copy to every client for whom type is assessed.*

Myers, I. B. (with Myers, P. B.). (1995). *Gifts differing: Understanding personality type.* Palo Alto, CA: Davies-Black.

*The classic Myers work, and her only book-length discussion of type. The book is a careful and straightforward explanation of Jung's theory as Myers and her mother, Katharine C. Briggs, interpreted and extended it. It provides the rationale and uses of type tables to understand type differences, the effects of each pair of preferences within a personality, and Myers's original descriptions of the 16 types. Myers covers the practical implications of type in marriage, early learning, learning styles, and occupations. Of particular value to clinicians is Myers's discussion of the importance of good type development in childhood and later, and how a person born with a disposition to develop along particular typological lines may have this development either enhanced or thwarted by life experiences such as parental type differences and the values and expectations of educational institutions.*

Myers, I. B., McCaulley, M. H., Quenk, N. L, & Hammer, A. L. (1998). *MBTI manual: A guide to the development and use of the Myers-Briggs Type Indicator.* Palo Alto, CA: Consulting Psychologists Press.

*This volume is the technical manual for the MBTI, providing a discussion of the history and development of the Jung / Myers theory, construction of MBTI forms that preceded Form M as well as construction of the current Form M; reliability and validity of previous forms and Form M; and research literature relevant to the validity of type constructs, in particular, evidence for the validity of whole types and type dynamics. Following the basic theory chapter is a lengthy chapter that gives descriptions of all 2-preference combinations and all 16 types, and includes tables summarizing research results relevant to each preference combination or whole type. The interpretive comments that follow each research table will be of particular importance to clinicians wanting insight into the impact of type on major areas of living. The comments provide specific ways in which the 16 types are not assessed or valued equally in important endeavors such as education, employment, and assessment of psychological and social adaptation.*

*   *This manual is also a comprehensive guide to applications of the MBTI in five main areas—couseling and psychotherapy, education, career counseling, organizations, and multicultural settings. Each of these five chapters was written by one or more expert in that area of application of the MBTI. The information provided in the application chapters covers both research relevant to the area as well as guidelines for using the MBTI in each setting. For example, a career counselor who has a basic knowledge of the MBTI such as is available in* Essentials of MBTI Assessment, *will be able to apply that knowledge based on the principles and guidelines that appear in the career counseling*

*chapter. The same is true for the other four application chapters. The extensive research in the validity chapter as well as in each application chapter supports the theoretical assumptions underlying type and contains a great deal of information that is relevant to clinical practice. Available knowledge for clinical applications is not limited to the counseling and psychotherapy chapter, however, as each of the other application chapters provide a wealth of insights relevant to treating individuals, couples, and families.*

Otis, G. D., & Louks, J. L. (1997). Rebelliousness and psychological distress in a sample of Introverted veterans. *Journal of Psychological Type, 40,* 20–30.

*An award-winning study that considered type dynamics in exploring the hypothesis that psychological dysfunction might emerge differently in different types. Though the study is limited in scope to male, Introverted veterans in an in-patient VA facility, the researchers found type-consistent differences in diagnoses and personal and social histories of sample members. Particularly notable is the authors' discussion of the results, which illustrates depth of understanding of the complexity and breadth of type and its clinical applications. This article serves as a model for in-depth clinical interpretation of research results in relation to the assessment of personality type.*

Provost, J. A. (1993). *Applications of the Myers-Briggs Type Indicator in counseling: A casebook.* Gainesville, FL: Center for Applications of Psychological Type.

*A revised edition of a work originally published in 1983. It provides a useful discussion of counseling applications of the MBTI and includes 18 case studies that show the impact of type on counseling issues and how counselors can apply type in their treatment of clients. A number of cases focus on young people in college and there is a helpful chapter on using type in counseling couples.*

Quenk, N. L. (1993). *Beside ourselves: Our hidden personality in everyday life.* Palo Alto, CA: Davies-Black.

*A comprehensive and enlightening discussion of how the inferior function is likely to be manifested in different types when they are experiencing any form of internal or external stress. It explains the dynamics of Jung's typology and why the eruption of the unconscious inferior function is a predictable, natural, and adaptive process that aids in the development of one's personality. Both clients and therapists will find the concepts and the many examples included to be helpful in understanding behavior that can seem unpredictable, puzzling, and upsetting. Clinicians might take special note of the likelihood that in their initial sessions with a client, they are likely to see the client's inferior function behavior, rather than a client operating out of his or her developed dominant and auxiliary functions.*

*This likelihood serves as a caution against assessing and diagnosing clients too early in the therapy process.*

Quenk, N. L. (1996). *In the Grip: Our hidden personality.*

*This is a brief, booklet-length version of* Beside Ourselves: Our Hidden Personality in Everyday Life, *by the same author. It is useful for students of type wanting a brief introduction to the meanings and manifestations of the inferior function in each of the types. In addition, it can be particularly helpful to counseling and psychotherapy clients who find themselves feeling and behaving in "out-of-character" ways during periods of stress or illness. Reading about the predictable nature of their sometimes frightening reactions can be calming and also encourage an examination of the life issues that may be stimulating inferior function reactions.*

Quenk, N. L., & Quenk, A. T. (1996). Counseling and psychotherapy. In A. L. Hammer (Ed.), *MBTI applications: A decade of research on the Myers-Briggs Type Indicator* (pp. 105–122). Palo Alto, CA: Consulting Psychologists Press.

*A review of research that was reported from 1984 to 1995, which includes a summary of previous research reported in the second edition of the MBTI manual (Myers & McCaulley, 1985). Research in seven areas is covered: preferred models of counseling and psychotherapy, relationship of type to supervision, type characteristics of users of psychological services, practitioner type and the therapeutic process, type and outcome of therapy, type and couples, type and substance abuse. The implications of these research results for practicing clinicians is discussed in comments concluding each section. Of particular interest to people wishing to do research on type that has clinical relevance is the discussion of the kind of studies needed in the field. The suggestions provide a wealth of research ideas for graduate students and professionals interested in contributing to this area.*

Thorne, A., & Gough, H. (1991). *Portraits of type: An MBTI research compendium.* Palo Alto, CA: Consulting Psychologists Press.

*The first major report of research that focused on whole types. Thorne and Gough compiled data collected over a number of years at the Institute for Personality Assessment and Research (IPAR) at the University of California, Berkeley. The IPAR samples consisted of 240 women and 374 men studied between 1956 and 1984 using the IPAR-intensive assessment method. Included were architects, mathematicians, students at various professional schools, and college students. The MBTI was one of the many assessment instruments used, in addition to the Adjective Check List (Gough & Heilbrun, 1983) the California Psychological Inventory (CPI), the Minnesota Multiphasic Personality*

*Inventory (MMPI) (Hathaway & McKinley, 1943), and the Block Q-sort, among others. Assessment techniques also included extensive ratings by trained observers. Sufficient data on 10 of the 16 types was available and includes several measures of psychological adjustment and various observer ratings, in addition to results of other instruments. Of particular relevance to clinicians is the fact that both subjects and observers did not know their own or each others' MBTI types, nor were they familiar with the concepts of type; self- and observer assessments are therefore from a general normative point of view. The descriptions of the whole types is in accord with summaries presented in the 1998 MBTI manual: Some types see themselves and are seen more and less favorably than other types, and are particularly notable when the gender of the types is taken into account.*

Wilson, M. A., & Languis, M. L. (1989). Differences in brain electrical activity patterns between introverted and extraverted adults. *Journal of Psychological Type, 18,* 14–23.

*The award-winning research that began an ongoing exploration of electrical activity pattern differences associated with opposite type preferences. The authors used topographic brain mapping technology to study Extraverts and Introverts with clear preferences on the MBTI. The results of this and subsequent studies strongly suggest that Extraversion and Introversion differences correspond to differences in the ways the brains of Extraverts and Introverts respond to identical stimulation. For a pictorial reproduction of such brain maps, see the MBTI manual (Myers et al., 1998, p. 190). Continuing research has also included differences between subjects with Sensing and Intuition preferences and combinations of Extraversion and Introversion with Sensing and Intuition.*

# Index

# Acknowledgments

Over the years, many colleagues, clients, friends, and family members have freely shared their personal and professional experiences with type. Without their insights, this book would not have been possible. I am particularly indebted to those psychotherapy clients who generously agreed to be included in the book as case examples. Nancy Barger and Linda Kirby read early drafts of the manuscript and provided helpful commentary. Joe Boggs, Sue Clancy, Karen Dorris, Jean Kummerow, Jan Mitchell, Roberta Rice, and Alex Quenk added important material and critiqued selected portions of the work. Their insights greatly improved the text.

I am most grateful to Jamelyn Johnson of the Center for Applications of Psychological Type, who provided helpful historical material, up-to-date information about the existing literature on psychological type, and composites of data from the CAPT databank.

I am most appreciative of the cooperation, support, and advice of Consulting Psychologists Press, publisher of the MBTI. Peggy Alexander, Senior Project Director for the MBTI, and Laura Ackerman-Shaw, Director of Design and Production, were especially helpful.

It was a pleasure working with Dorothy Lin, Associate Editor at John Wiley & Sons, and Series Editors Alan and Nadeen Kaufman, all of whom offered excellent comments and suggestions that improved and enhanced the chapters. The editing of Kim Nir, Managing Editor, and Tammi Brooks, who oversaw production of the book, added clarity and consistency to the work.

## About the Author

Naomi L. Quenk is a clinical psychologist in independent practice in Albuquerque, New Mexico. She was introduced to the MBTI in 1960 as a graduate student at the University of California, Berkeley, and has incorporated typology into many aspects of her work ever since. She has contributed a wide range of articles and several books that focus on theory, research, and clinical and other applications of psychological type. She is the author of *Beside Ourselves: Our Hidden Personality in Everyday Life* and *In the Grip: Our Hidden Personality*. She coauthored the *Interpretive Guide for the MBTI Expanded Analysis Report* and *Workbook for the MBTI Expanded Analysis Report,* the *MBTI Step II Expanded Interpretive Report,* and most recently, the current revision of the MBTI manual, *Manual: A Guide to the Development and Use of the Myers-Briggs Type Indicator*. She is a past president of the Association for Psychological Type and directed the association's MBTI Qualifying Training program for many years. In addition, she serves on the Myers-Briggs Research Advisory Board and is a director of the Myers & Briggs Foundation.